THE INNOVATION FORGE

How to Build, Automate, and Strategically Use Engagement Scoring and Predictive Modeling in the Slate CRM

David Dysart

CONTENTS

ACT I: ENGAGEMENT SCORING

Acknowledgments

Neither I nor ChatGPT could come up with the proper words to express my gratitude to everyone with ties to this book. I will try (and keep it brief).

My wonderful wife and amazing son - Constant inspirations every day in all things. And patient ones at that - at least my wife. Taking recommendations on how to teach a 2-year old patience.

My friends and family - That have given me such a beautiful life and helped craft how I think of and view the world.

Every colleague, client, boss, and giants in the fields I have studied, worked in, or have spilled into my life somehow - Like a snowball rolling down a long and winding hill, I've picked up so many things from everyone. And I wouldn't be the slushy ball of wet snow otherwise.

Reader(s?) - Despite my fascination to cling onto shiny projects, I am writing this and tinkering with new projects because I am hopeful they can help someone. Whether that's a staff member whose life is easier or better for having learned something or a student whose experience is better as a result of the project. So you have my utmost gratitude for spending your time reading these words. I hope they help you on your journey.

Thank you. For a full heart and a full book. Full-ish at least. As someone who has written hundreds of thousands of words of fiction as a hobby, I never thought my first book would be a guide for higher education.

Though this was not my first attempt at a higher education book. I had spun into start-stop cycles a couple of times trying to write a book specifically on using Slate by Technolutions. The scope of the book, rapid evolution of Slate, and nearly non-Euclidean sprawl of the system to touch so many functions on campus always stymied my efforts.

A series of the books on projects that lend themselves well to Slate but are applicable to other systems made much more sense. At least that seems to be the case as I type this out. This book was not even meant to be a book. I had initially written 6 accompanying articles to be supporting documentation for a 6-part series of Workshops on Engagement Scoring and Predictive

Modeling. But as a wise mouth once said, the words start coming, and they don't stop coming.

The Journey Begins

Oh Scoring. Engagement Scoring as a project spent so much time on the backburner. I had been wanting to do it since the quaint, Halcyon days that were the Slate Template Library before Configurable Joins. Can I use BC? Is that taken already? Maybe BCJ? Scoring though seemed complicated and was always a "Next Summer Project".

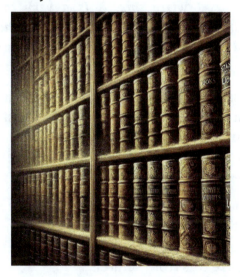

Surely I'm not the only one with Next Summer Projects, am I? They feel like college athletes waiting for the NFL draft. I discuss the team needs with leadership, and we end up drafting the long snapper that will support the office in a mission-critical way. Look, no offense, Mr. Kelce. You're an amazing player and locker room presence, but tight ends are more exciting on the ESPN highlight reels (and apparently for pop stars).

Author's Note: as I write this, it is a very topical reference. Inevitably, whenever you read it, it won't be. You have my sincerest apologies. And realistically, this will not be my only football tangent. I will make an honest effort to limit those though.

Well, Scoring sat undrafted for years. I even tried delegating the lift to other staff when Configurable Joins first came in (does delegation count as signing a free agent? Can I just stop this metaphor at this point? Would that be dropping the ball? Let me know).

Then came the COVID-19 Pandemic (I imagine a much more memorable reference) and the many, many projects required to convert our operations in response. Definitely not the time to start a project like this from scratch.

Enter (or Exit I suppose) Slate Predict. This was a non-functional page in Slate about leveraging predictive analytics in an instance of Slate. While it was never (as far as I could tell) working, I was always excited for it. Then it just disappeared in 2021.

I took a step back. Why would I continue to wait for Slate to build a Predictive Modeling tool? I know how to build models. And as soon as I built the model, I could (at least in the amorphous shroud that is first formulations of a project) actually build the model into Slate to keep the records updated in near real time.

But if this did not have the biggest "Next Summer Project" energy, I did not know what would. The sheer scale of data cleanup (and extraction), feature engineering, statistical model building, the technical build in Slate (including getting VERY cozy with Configurable Joins), and what could be a never-ending scaffolding of the uses of such a project in the policy, practices, and strategy of my institution at the time. I wish I didn't already use my "non-Euclidean" reference in this chapter. Let's just say this is the kind of project that "sleeps" in R'lyeh, and I feared for my sanity if I woke it.

But who needs something as pedestrian as sanity? So I buckled in and took the dive at the end of summer 2021. Join me for this tale of 3 acts.

CHAPTER 1: UNDERSTANDING ENGAGEMENT SCORING IN SLATE

The Customer Relationship Management System

In the rapidly evolving landscape of higher education, institutions are increasingly turning to technology to streamline their operations, enhance student engagement, and improve decision-making. Most commonly, a CRM or Customer Relationship Management system is used. This book will use Slate from Technolutions as this platform. It's the system I'm most familiar with and the one that I used to develop these processes. It offers an array of tools to track student interactions across various touchpoints. From communications and event participation to portal logins, Slate captures a wealth of data that can be used to assess student engagement and be the platform for those engagements. Its ability to easily ingest data from other systems increases the scope of data an institution can use to create Scores and Models. Configurable Joins also provide robust feature engineering abilities.

While it started as a system for higher ed Admission offices, it continues to expand into Student Success and Advancement offices and even position itself as a critical element of a System of Systems approach that could include and replace a Student Information System (SIS) altogether. If I was to pitch its use outside of a college to you now, it would not be my first time. Nor would it be the first time Slate was used outside of an institution of higher education.

Now, this book is not an #ad. (Author's note: Technolutions... It could be. Send me a Deliver. You have my cell phone number and email already. And just look at any of my Dahveed Testy Test accounts across several of your clients. That's my... personal email.)

Poorly placed influencer attempts aside, Slate does provide an excellent platform for these and other projects. With a bit of tinkering, there are many other valid options you could use and implement Engagement Scoring and Predictive Modeling. Use this book as a guide on your "choose your own adventure" path.

Similarly, the strategies, data, and references in this book primarily use the admission office. But these can be easily translated to other offices and uses. For consistency, ease, and my ever questionable sanity, I'll refer to Admissions typically.

There are some key elements that will be needed both for Engagement Scoring and crucial to support the student lifecycle, from recruitment to alumnae relations. Some of the features include:

1. **Data Management and Integration**: Slate allows you to centralize data, integrating easily with existing systems such as Student Information Systems (SIS)

and Learning Management Systems (LMS) as well as vendor and other data sources. This integration facilitates a holistic view of each student's journey, ensuring that relevant information is accessible and actionable.

2. **Communication Tools**: With Slate, you can automate and personalize communication with prospective, current, and former students. It offers a suite of tools for email marketing, SMS, virtual experience interactions, and website tracking allowing for targeted messaging based on student behaviors, preferences, and data.

3. **Event Management**: Slate simplifies the organization and management of events such as campus tours, open houses, and informational sessions. It tracks student participation and engagement, providing valuable data that can inform future recruitment strategies.

4. **Application Management**: The platform streamlines the application process, offering customizable forms and workflows that can be tailored to the specific needs of each institution. This feature helps your team manage applications efficiently and effectively.

5. **Analytics and Reporting**: Slate provides powerful analytics and reporting tools that allow you to track key performance indicators and measure the effectiveness of recruitment and retention efforts. This data-driven approach enables you to make informed decisions and adjust strategies as needed. While these tools are great in-system, many institutions do use external reporting and visualization software.

At its core, Slate is designed to enhance student engagement by providing tools you use to understand and respond to student needs. By capturing a wide net of data on student interactions, from email communications and event participation to portal logins and application submissions, Slate empowers institutions to build strong, meaningful relationships with their students.

Engagement Scores

In the context of higher education, Engagement Scoring represents a transformative approach to understanding and leveraging student data. Engagement Scoring involves quantifying a student's interactions with an institution to gauge their level of interest and involvement. This Score can be used to inform recruitment strategies, empower marketing and communications, prioritize resources, and enhance decision-making in admissions.

One of the primary benefits of Engagement Scoring is its ability to transform raw data into actionable insights. Institutions often collect vast amounts of data on prospective, current, and former students, but without a structured approach to analyzing this data, its potential remains untapped. Engagement Scoring provides a framework for systematically evaluating student behaviors and translating them into meaningful metrics and guide strategy.

Act III of this book uses several frameworks on how Engagement Scoring and Predictive Modeling can be used at your institution. If you have already built these tools or want to learn more about how you can use them, I won't take it personally. I promise. Pinky promise.

Scoring Development

Your institution may call this concept something else. Demonstrated Interest, Affinity, Lead Scoring. But all roads are leading to the development of a Score to understand your student and guide the institution. By analyzing behaviors such as event attendance, email communication, and portal activity, institutions can assess the strength of a student's interest and use this information to inform recruitment and admissions decisions.

To develop an effective Engagement Scoring model or rubric, you must determine how to weight and combine these behaviors into a cohesive Score. This process involves assigning point values to each behavior based on its perceived importance and relevance to demonstrated interest. For example, attending an on-campus event might be worth more points than opening an email, reflecting the higher level of commitment required.

Every institution is unique, and Engagement Scoring rubrics should be customized to reflect the specific priorities and goals of each college or university. By involving admissions staff and other stakeholders in the development of the Scoring model, you can ensure that the system aligns with your institution's strategic objectives and provides meaningful insights into student engagement.

With that in mind, historical data will be a (if not the) primary driver of this Scoring rubric. Provided the institution has consistent historical data to pull from and some kind of outcome metric like staff evaluation of interest, application flag, or enrollment flag, then this Score can begin integrating into your institution's practices.

Slate provides the tools necessary to automate the Engagement Scoring process, allowing institutions to efficiently capture and analyze student interactions. By leveraging Slate's Queries and Source Formats, you can create a dynamic Scoring system that updates in a practical schedule, providing admissions teams with the most current information on student engagement.

Behaviors

To effectively Score engagement, you have to identify and track key behaviors that indicate interest. Some behaviors to monitor include:

Event Attendance: Participating in events, whether virtual or in-person, is a strong indicator of a student's interest in an institution. Tracking attendance at events such as campus tours, open houses, and informational sessions can provide valuable insights into a student's level of engagement.

> **Author's Note**: It is important that accessible events are created and tracked so a high score is not simply a proxy for able and high socioeconomic status of prospective students who had the time and resources to visit campuses. Videos of your events, live virtual events, and virtual experience portals can all provide a high fidelity view of the campus and student experience while also complimenting on-campus programming. Additional Bonuses covered later in this book may help you balance accessibility in your Scoring.

Email Communication: The frequency and content of email communication between a student and the institution can reveal important information about their interest and intent. Analyzing email interactions can help identify students who are actively seeking information and are more likely to apply and enroll.

> **Author's Note**: With privacy protections diminishing the validity of engagement statistics by students, it is important to remove the noise from these kinds of behaviors. It's also key to count emails from the student, not other emails that may be getting attached to their Slate record like counselor emails and documents. The Feature Engineering Chapter later will detail this.

Portal Activity: Logging into the student portal to access resources, submit applications, or check application status is another key indicator of engagement. Frequent portal activity suggests that a student is actively considering the institution and is engaged in the admissions process. This can be even more predictive when a parent/copilot portal is built and engaged with.

> **Author's Note**: Some students may apply and fulfill all requirements without much virtual engagement. With Ping tracking on the institution's website, similar engagement metrics can be considered. Prospective students with limited time or virtual access to engage with your institution may also be hindered with these metrics.

Application Progress: Tracking a student's progress through the application process, including the submission of required materials and responses to application prompts, can provide insights into their commitment to attending the institution.

> **Author's Note**: A lot of "Feature Engineering" can go into this. More often seen in Predictive Modeling, it is the process of selecting, modifying, or creating new variables (features). It involves identifying key data attributes that can enhance your power by transforming or combining existing data into more meaningful representations. Instead of assigning points for submitting a required document, how long after application or Slate record creation did it happen?

Rubric

Once the key behaviors have been identified, the next step is to assign point values to each action. This process involves determining the relative importance of each behavior and its contribution to the overall Engagement Score (and appropriate subscores like Event, MarComm, etc.). For example, attending an in-person event might be worth more points than attending a virtual event, reflecting the higher level of commitment required.

To ensure that the Scoring system aligns with institutional priorities, it's essential you involve admissions officers and other stakeholders in the process of assigning point values. This collaborative approach helps ensure that the Scoring model accurately reflects the institution's strategic objectives and provides meaningful insights into student engagement.

Collaborative Scoring will be crucial if you implement a new process, project, or way to engage with the institution that you don't have historical data to inform Scoring. This early collaboration also sets the stage for the eventual use in the office as staff members are already engaged with a sense of ownership in the process and tool.

Any Scoring rubric should also be highly informed by the institution's historical data. I have found Excel to be an invaluable tool in this process as it's much faster for me to include, score, and validate behaviors there than Slate. Both collaboration and historical data Modeling will be covered in greater details in the following chapters.

Conclusion

Engagement Scoring in Slate offers a powerful framework for understanding and enhancing student engagement in higher education. By transforming raw data into actionable insights, Engagement Scoring enables you to tailor your recruitment strategies, prioritize applicants, and make informed decisions in admissions. As institutions continue to navigate the challenges and opportunities of the digital age, Engagement Scoring will play a crucial role in building meaningful relationships with students and driving success across the student lifecycle.

In the following chapters, we will get more into technical details of building and automating Engagement Scoring systems in Slate, explore the role of Predictive Modeling in higher education, and provide practical guidance for leveraging these tools to achieve institutional goals with what I call Adaptive Enrollment Management.

CHAPTER 2: COLLABORATION AND STAFF ENGAGEMENT

Before we wander into the weeds of building the Engagement Score rubric, we should take from to discuss collaboration. It goes without saying that decisions need data behind them, driving your institution forward, but that represents one piece of the equation. The expertise and nuanced understanding of your institution and students are crucial in building the Score, advancing data, and meeting institutional goals.

So let's explore the balance between staff and data insights. The approach and culture of getting your staff involved and gathering their qualitative insights will be crucial in keeping them engaged and contributing to this and other projects. It will also set the stage for them to fully integrate the Score into their day-to-day as well as their strategy. This all paves a path that leads you not only to institutional success, but student success as well.

With tools like Slate, you can create a frictionless and well-informed environment for projects to be created. And with the collaboration of your team, they understand how this project will build them a tool that allows them to focus the human work, not replace them with a machine or algorithm. And by facilitating genuine two-way communication and feedback, you can begin to build an adaptable culture of improvement that can respond to change and needs.

Balancing Data And Expertise

In today's data-driven world, higher education institutions are increasingly relying on sophisticated analytics to inform their recruitment and admissions strategies. However, while data-driven insights are invaluable, they must be complemented by the experience and knowledge of admissions officers and other staff members. Balancing these two elements is crucial for developing an Engagement Scoring system that aligns with institutional goals and effectively supports recruitment efforts.

Incorporating staff and stakeholders at this stage also increases buy-in from them. For these Scores and Models to become integrated into your institution's practices and used in meaningful ways, staff will not only need to want to use the final tools, but to craft their strategic approach to work with them. The institution does not simply flip a light switch after implementation and everything changes overnight.

Institutions that will benefit the most from these tools will be the ones who take the time to thoughtfully build, integrate, and utilize them. With the sense of ownership and contribution that comes from working on the tools at this stage, staff will be far more likely to use and continue to improve them later.

But not to worry. We'll dive headlong into the data and gears of your historical data later in this book.

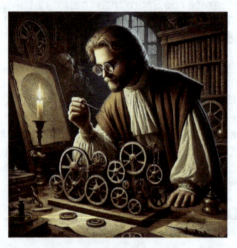

Data In Higher Education

Data has become a cornerstone of strategic decision-making in higher education. Institutions are collecting vast amounts of information on prospective and current students, ranging from academic performance and demographic data to engagement metrics and behavioral indicators. This data provides valuable insights into student preferences and behaviors, enabling you to tailor your recruitment strategies and improve the effectiveness of their admissions processes.

However, relying solely on data can have limitations. Data-driven models may not always capture the nuances of human behavior or account for the unique context of individual students. There may also be limitations to the availability, use, and integrity of the data. Admissions officers possess valuable insights gained through years of experience working with students and your data. Their expertise allows them to identify patterns and trends that may not be immediately apparent from the existing data alone.

This is even more important as the tools, tracking, and offerings in Slate constantly evolve, and your institution's use of it changes along with it. A great instance of Slate does not look exactly like it did "today - 1 year" ago.

Staff Expertise

Admissions officers and other staff members bring a wealth of experience and knowledge to the table. They have firsthand experience interacting with students and understanding their motivations, challenges, and aspirations. This expertise is invaluable in shaping recruitment strategies and ensuring that the Engagement Scoring system reflects the institution's priorities. And if the Engagement Score was purely meant to be correlated with a particular outcome like applying or enrolling, then we could simply skip to Predictive Modeling.

1. **Contextual Understanding**: Staff members have a deep understanding of the institution's culture, values, and strategic goals. This context is crucial for interpreting data and making informed decisions

about recruitment and admissions.

2. **Student Interactions**: Admissions officers have direct interactions with students and can provide insights into their needs and preferences. This firsthand experience allows staff to identify factors that may influence a student's decision to apply or enroll. This becomes increasingly crucial when further developing the CRM to codify, track, or integrate these factors.

3. **Institutional Knowledge**: Staff members possess institutional knowledge that can help guide the development of the Engagement Scoring system. They understand the unique characteristics of the student population and can provide valuable input on which behaviors and interactions should be prioritized in the Scoring model.

Balancing Data And Expertise Reprise

To create an effective Engagement Scoring system, you must strike a balance between data-driven insights and staff expertise. This balance ensures that the Scoring model is both accurate and relevant, reflecting the institution's goals and priorities.

Collaborative Development: Involving staff in the development of the Engagement Scoring system ensures that their expertise is integrated into the model. By working together, data analysts and admissions officers can create a Scoring system that reflects the institution's strategic objectives and provides meaningful insights into student engagement.

Continuous Feedback: Establishing feedback mechanisms allows staff to provide input on the Scoring model and suggest improvements. Regularly soliciting feedback from staff ensures that the system remains relevant and responsive to changing needs.

Data-Driven Decision-Making: While staff expertise is invaluable, data-driven insights provide a more objective basis for decision-making. By combining data with expert input, you can make more informed and equitable decisions about recruitment and admissions.

Staff Involvement

Effective communication is key to successful collaboration. You can use a variety of tools and platforms to facilitate communication and gather feedback from staff, ensuring that their input is integrated into the Scoring model.

Slate Forms, Delivers, and Portals: Slate offers a range of tools for facilitating communication and collaboration. Slate Forms and Portals allow staff to provide feedback on the Scoring model, suggest improvements, and track the progress of the project. These platforms enable real-time communication and ensure that all stakeholders are informed and engaged in the process.

Workshops and Training Sessions: Hosting workshops and training sessions can help build consensus and understanding among staff. These sessions provide an opportunity for staff to learn about the Engagement Scoring system, ask questions, and provide input on its development. Workshops also serve as a platform for sharing best practices and discussing potential challenges.

Regular Meetings and Check-Ins: Regular meetings and check-ins with staff ensure that the project stays on track and that any issues are addressed promptly. These meetings provide an opportunity for staff to share their insights and discuss any concerns they may have about the Scoring model.

Fostering a culture of collaboration is essential for the success of any project. By encouraging open communication and collaboration, institutions can create an environment where staff feel empowered to contribute their expertise and insights.

Leadership support is crucial for fostering a culture of collaboration. Leaders should communicate the importance of collaboration and provide the resources and support needed to facilitate it. By Modeling collaborative behavior, leaders can encourage staff to engage in the process and contribute their insights.

Recognizing and rewarding staff for their contributions to the Engagement Scoring system can help reinforce a collaborative culture. By celebrating successes and acknowledging the efforts of staff, institutions can create a positive and supportive environment that encourages collaboration.

Also encouraging a culture of continuous improvement ensures that the Engagement Scoring system remains relevant and effective. By regularly reviewing and updating the Scoring model based on feedback and new data, institutions can ensure that it continues to support recruitment efforts and align with institutional goals.

Providing a Slate Architecture

I wanted to further highlight some tools and ideas for using Slate to collaborate.

Forms:

There will likely be multiple rounds of idea generation, feedback, and refinement. Using a tool like Slate Forms allows these responses to be tied to the person and serve as an iterative reference.

From collecting behaviors to include, "red flags" and negative points, bonuses, and recommending points and distributions, Slate offers a clean and effective data collection tool for most projects.

Engagement Scoring

What behaviors demonstrate an "engaged" student?

What Red Flags do you see when evaluating applications (e.g. Event No-Shows)?

Scoring

In-Person Events: Points Per Behavior

In-Person Events: Maximum Points

{{'mobile_template_internal' : snippet: "header"}}

Hi {{Preferred}},

We are still collecting feedback on our new Engagement Scoring process.
Please let us know by MM/dd/yy for us to incorporate your input into the pilot.

You can review our current scoring rubric and additional details at {{project_link}}.

Sincerely,

{{'director' | snippet: "signature_image"}}

It's also a good place to build a "Request a Meeting" feature. At the end of the form, I usually add a field about requesting a meeting and additional text box for questions. The Form Communication then emails me to schedule the meeting. A link to Active Scheduler or some other meeting system would also work.

Form responses should be tied to the participants in some capacity (unless you want anonymous responses). The fast and easy way is to just use Slate-delivered records. Throw a Test Tag on them, and use a Form to track datapoints like Role, Office, Title, etc.

Pictured Above: Our daring Quickster boldly doing things fast and easy regardless of the intentions of his slippery foe: Downstream Consequences

I've found Slate-ifying these records helps with multiple projects and Staff Delivers. So I would not utilize the User records as many staff that could be used in this process won't need associated User accounts.

That said, a standalone Dataset would be more robust and have less downstream consequences. But it requires the time and exposure (or willingness to do get familiar) with Datasets.

Pro Tip: Add Export Keys to your forms to use the data in Deliver, Queries, etc.

Even if you're not sure if you'll pull together or aggregate the form responses, you may need to, so being proactive before the dreaded "Downstream Consequences" strikes is always a good call.

You can add Export Keys to your fields or connecting directly to Slate fields will also make responses much easier to use. We will cover one of these uses in the Deliver section. Multi-select in Configurable Joins will be unpleasant, but that's another issue.

Deliver:

I like using a standalone Deliver to send updates/requests to staff. The email body can contain a curated email chain so every email to staff can be used as a reference to the project.

Paired with the standalone staff records covered above, the emails are also synced with the records and can use person-specific links with a GUID.

It would look something like adding this to the end of the URL: "&person={{Person-GUID}}".

This also requires creating a custom URL for your form. Otherwise, you would add "?person={{Person-GUID}}".

For the first parameter of a URL, it starts with a "?", which Slate will use with the default Form URL. Subsequent parameters use "&". As a Slate Captain, I generally recommended all Forms to use a custom URL so staff did not have to try to figure out when to use "?" versus a "&" to prefill forms with student data.

And since we added Export Codes to the Forms (or connected Form Fields to Slate Fields), we can add person-specific, aggregate, and other specific responses to the email.

In this screenshot, staff used the form to recommend how many points they would score (e.g. 15 points per event) and a maximum points available (e.g. total of 75 points possible)

The Deliver will generate a person-specific email to send to each staff that lists their responses as a dependent subquery export. But it also contextualizes responses by giving averages from all (or subset like counselors, leadership, etc.) responses with an independent subquery export. Examples of the email and independent subquery below.

Hi David,

Here are the current Averages (with your score in parentheses) from the Feedback Form:

In-Person Event
Points: 10 (15)
Maximum: 47.5 (75)

You can updated your feedback on our new Engagement Scoring process until MM/dd/yy.

You can review our current scoring rubric and additional details at our project hub.

Sincerely,

David Dysart
Director of Data and Functional Systems Design
Beyond Academics

Portal:

The same kinds of information and updates being embedded in a Deliver can also be plugged into a Staff Portal. This comes with several added benefits. As projects start, Portal content can be added to some or all staff members' Portal. If there's an action item, then once they complete it, that content can be removed/updated to show their completion. New action items or updates can float the content back to staff so they can stay informed and involved.

Institutional Outcomes

The collaborative approach to developing the Engagement Scoring system results in several positive outcomes for the college:

Improved Recruitment Strategies: The Engagement Scoring model rooted in an institution-specific rubric provides valuable insights into student interest and allows your institution to tailor its recruitment strategies accordingly. By identifying high-potential prospects, the admissions team is able to focus its efforts on students who were most likely to apply and enroll.

Increased Staff Engagement: Involving staff in the development process fosters a sense of ownership and commitment to the project. Staff feel empowered to contribute their expertise and are more engaged in using the Score and integrating it into the recruitment process as a result.

Continuous Improvement: The collaborative process establishes a foundation for continuous improvement, ensuring that the Scoring model remains relevant and effective. By regularly soliciting feedback from staff and updating the model based on new data, you are able to maintain its effectiveness in supporting recruitment efforts.

Conclusion

Developing an effective Engagement Scoring system in Slate requires a collaborative approach that balances data-driven insights with staff expertise. By involving staff in the process and leveraging their knowledge and experience, you can create a Scoring Model that aligns with your strategic goals and effectively supports recruitment efforts.

Collaboration is key to the success of any project, and institutions must foster a culture of collaboration that encourages open communication and engagement. By facilitating communication and feedback, encouraging collaboration across departments, and recognizing the contributions of staff, you can develop an Engagement Scoring system that reflects the needs and priorities of the entire institution.

The following chapters will explore the technical details of using historical data and automating Engagement Scoring systems in Slate. Afterwards, we will discuss Predictive Modeling and how to integrate both Scoring and Modeling into your processes and leverage these tools to achieve student and institutional success.

CHAPTER 3: EXCEL FOR SCORING AND VALIDATION

In the realm of higher education, data-driven decision-making is becoming increasingly essential to optimize recruitment strategies and improve student engagement.

Slate does a wonderful job facilitating that, but data exploration, Scoring comparison, and validation can be easier out of the system. I have found Excel to be an exceptional tool for analyzing historical data, Scoring behaviors, and validating them to an existing variable like a staff evaluation or if the student applied and enrolled.

Similarly, our previous chapter on utilizing staff knowledge is a wonderful starting place to understand the data available and how your institution views their students in context of engagement behaviors. It may even lead to new data collection and practices. It will also likely spark variable selection and feature engineering that may have been missed by starting with a Slate Query. But that is the starting point in the path to create an Engagement Score. The rubric will largely be driven by historical data analysis.

This chapter focuses on providing step-by-step instructions for using Excel in Scoring and validation.

Using Excel For Data Exploration And Scoring

Excel is a versatile tool that can be used to manage and analyze large data sets, making it invaluable for Engagement Scoring and validation. With its robust functionality, Excel allows you to explore data, apply Scoring logic, and validate results against historical data and other variables.

Step 1: Importing Data

The first step in using Excel for Engagement Scoring is importing data from your CRM. This could include interactions like event attendance, email communications, and portal logins, into a CSV or Excel file. The process to build these data exports is essentially the same as building them to automate the Scoring process in Slate, so I will defer to that chapter to dive into the Configurable Joins building.

Once your Query has been built, export to generate a file containing relevant student data. Ensure that all necessary data points for Scoring are included in the export. You will want the counts of these behaviors. Not any kind of Scoring at this point.

At this point, you can use this file to build your analysis document or move data into that file. As part of my 6-part

Workshop Series, I created an Excel document that can be used and adapted for your project.

Slate recently released a live sync feature to quickly update the records in your file with current Slate data. If you haven't done this yet, Technolutions has created an Excel-lent video walking through the steps.

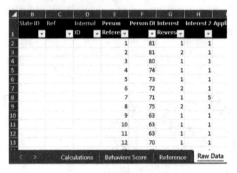

	B	C	D	E	F	G	H
	Slate ID	Ref	Internal ID	Person Refere	Person DI Interest	Interest 2 Revers	Appl
1							
2				1	81	1	1
3				2	81	2	1
4				3	80	1	1
5				4	74	1	1
6				5	73	1	1
7				6	72	2	1
8				7	71	1	5
9				8	75	2	1
10				9	63	1	1
11				10	63	1	1
12				11	63	1	1
13				12	70	1	1

Calculations | Behaviors Score | Reference | Raw Data

Step 2: Cleaning and Preparing Data

Once the data is imported, it is essential to clean and prepare it for analysis. This step includes removing duplicates, handling missing values (if not accounted for in the Slate Exports), and formatting columns for consistency.

Step 3: Assigning Point Values

Next, assign point values to each behavior based on its importance in indicating student engagement. This step involves creating formulas to calculate Engagement Scores for each student.

Create a Scoring Matrix: In a separate tab, create a Scoring matrix that lists each behavior and its corresponding point value. This matrix serves as a reference for the formulas calculating Scores.

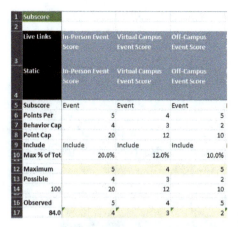

	Subscore			
1	Subscore			
2				
3	Live Links	In-Person Event Score	Virtual Campus Event Score	Off-Campus Event Score
	Static	In-Person Event Score	Virtual Campus Event Score	Off-Campus Event Score
4				
5	Subscore	Event	Event	Event	
6	Points Per	5	4	5
7	Behavior Cap	4	3	2
8	Point Cap	20	12	10
9	Include	Include	Include	Include	
10	Max % of Tot	20.0%	12.0%	10.0%
12	Maximum	5	4	5
13	Possible	4	3	2
14	100	20	12	10
16	Observed	5	4	5
17	84.0	4	3	2

This tab is the control hub to build the new Engagement Score. By creating corresponding columns for each of the Slate Exports, you can more easily apply and update the process.

1. An "Include" cell allows you to include and remove behaviors as you build the Score (and assign subscore categories).

2. Additional cells to assign the number of points and the maximum allowed points per behavior.

3. An additional tab will apply the points and create the Engagement Score for each historical record. But this tab will leverage records to describe the observed dataset like the maximum number of possible points and the actual highest Score achieved by your records.

Use Formulas to Calculate Scores: Use Excel formulas to calculate Engagement Scores based on the behaviors and point values.

=IFERROR(IF(('Raw Data'!T2*Reference!T$6) >=Reference!T$8, Reference!T$8, ('Raw Data'!T2*Reference!T$6)), 0)

This formula does several things:

1. If this formula produces an error, instead of breaking (and Downstream Consequences showing up), Excel

33

will return a 0. While building, replace the "0" with another value so you can catch and adjust errors.

2. If the number of behaviors exceed the prescribed maximum allotted points in the Scoring rubric, then only grant the maximum allotted points.

3. Provided neither of those issues happened, multiply the number of behaviors a student performed by the Scoring rubric's points per behavior.

Step 4: Aggregating Engagement Scores

| | SUMIF | | X ✓ fx | =ROUND(SUMIFS($B6:$DO6, $B$2:$DO$2, "Include")+ SUMIFS($B6:$DO6, $B$2:$DO$2, "Bonus"), 0) | | | | | |

	A		J	K		T	U	V	W	X
1										
2	Include		Bonus	Bonus		Include	Include	Include	Include	Include
3	Subscore		Engagement	Engagement		Event	Event	Event	Event	Engagement
	Automat ed Score		Bonus 1	Bonus 2		Behavior 1	Behavior 2	Behavior 3	Behavior 4	Behavior 5
4										
6	0)		2.8	7.3		15	12	10	1	6
7	80.0		2.8	7.3		15	12	10	1	6
8	82.0		2.8	7.6		20	8	10	2	6
9	70.0		2.4	6.3		5	12	10	2	6
10	81.0		2.8	7.4		15	12	10	2	6
11	63.0		2.1	5.7		15	12	0	1	6

Once Scores are calculated for individual behaviors, aggregate them into a total Engagement Score for each student. This step involves summing the scores across all behaviors.

After each behavior is scored, create an Engagement Score by summing each of those behaviors

=ROUND(SUMIFS($B6:$DO6, $B$2:$DO$2, "Include") +SUMIFS($B6:$DO6, $B$2:$DO$2, "Bonus"), 0)

This formula does several things:

1. At this point, I'm interested in rounding to whole numbers. This may or may not be needed in your process. This is largely a result of certain "bonuses" I've created.

2. Sum all scored behaviors from my dataset IF:

3. I marked them to "Include" in my Scoring rubric.

4. Sum all "bonuses" that I've included in my dataset. We will discuss this in a later chapter.

Step 5: Validating and Refining Scores

Validation is a critical step in ensuring the accuracy and reliability of Engagement Scores. This process involves comparing scores to historical data and refining the Scoring model as needed.

Use Excel to compare Engagement Scores to historical datapoints like staff evaluations or application or enrollment behaviors. This comparison helps assess the effectiveness of the Scoring Model.

Based on the validation results, refine the point values and formulas used in the Scoring Model. Adjust point values to better reflect the importance of each behavior.

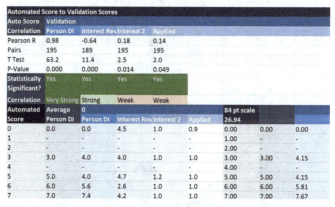

Automated Score to Validation Scores								
Auto Score	**Validation**							
Correlation	**Person DI**	**Interest Rev**	**Interest 2**	**Applied**				
Pearson R	0.98	-0.64	0.18	0.14				
Pairs	195	189	195	195				
T Test	63.2	11.4	2.5	2.0				
P-Value	0.000	0.000	0.014	0.049				
Statistically Significant?	Yes	Yes	Yes	Yes				
Correlation	Very Strong	Strong	Weak	Weak				
Automated	**Average**	0				84 pt scale		
Score	**Person DI**	**Person DI**	**Interest Rev**	**Interest 2**	**Applied**	26.94		
0	0.0	0.0	4.5	1.0	0.9	0.00	0.00	0.00
1	-	-	-	-	-	1.00	-	-
2	-	-	-	-	-	2.00	-	-
3	3.0	4.0	4.0	1.0	1.0	3.00	3.00	4.15
4	-	-	-	-	-	4.00	-	-
5	5.0	4.0	4.7	1.2	1.0	5.00	5.00	4.15
6	6.0	5.6	2.6	1.0	1.0	6.00	6.00	5.81
7	7.0	7.4	4.2	1.0	1.0	7.00	7.00	7.67

This entire Excel document is essentially built so we can evaluate this tab. The Scoring process is automated, so as points per behavior changes or different behavior data is used, Excel shows how it affects the behaviors, relationships, and Score.

This dissects each behavior to the possible value (where that Round formula comes in handy). It then maps empirical observations in your historical dataset of what the average validation values are for each.

For example, students whose new automated Engagement Score is a 5 have (on average) a 4.7 Staff Demonstrated Interest Review Form evaluation, 1.2 "Interest" in the Interview, and apply 100% percent of the time.

This helps to visualize trends in the data and where correlations are stronger and where they start to break down.

More importantly, you need to know how correlated the new Engagement Score is with your validation variables. This is where the ease of Excel starts to differentiate itself from doing this data exploration in Slate. Everything up to this point would have been time consuming to build in Slate (and probably lengthy to generate in a report every time you updated the Scoring rubric), not to mention taking up a lot of visual real estate, but it is reasonable and doable.

Your next step in Excel though is to run a Pearson R comparison between your new automated Engagement Score and the validation variables. Now before you blanch at using statistics, look at how cute our little Pearson is!

Don't worry. Excel will run the analysis and has the tables built in to determine statistical significance and effect size. And we'll use some rules of thumb to play red light, green light to make evaluation easier.

Note from our resident Field of Statistics Mouse: A Chi Square Test (CHISQ.TEST in Excel) is the appropriate statistic for your categorical variables. But we'll just use Pearson R for this book. CORREL is a similar function and may save some rounding errors compared to Pearson R, particularly for older versions of Excel.

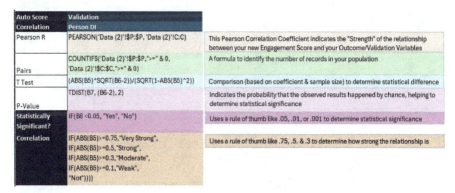

Auto Score	Validation	
Correlation	Person DI	
Pearson R	PEARSON('Data (2)'!$P:$P, 'Data (2)'!C:C)	This Pearson Correlation Coefficient indicates the "Strength" of the relationship between your new Engagement Score and your Outcome/Validation Variables
Pairs	COUNTIFS('Data (2)'!$P:$P,">=" & 0, 'Data (2)'!$C:$C,">=" & 0)	A formula to identify the number of records in your population
T Test	(ABS(B5)*SQRT(B6-2))/(SQRT(1-ABS(B5)^2))	Comparison (based on coefficient & sample size) to determine statistical difference
P-Value	TDIST(B7, (B6-2), 2)	Indicates the probability that the observed results happened by chance, helping to determine statistical significance
Statistically Significant?	IF(B8 <0.05, "Yes", "No")	Uses a rule of thumb like .05, .01, or .001 to determine statistical significance
Correlation	IF(ABS(B5)>=0.75,"Very Strong", IF(ABS(B5)>=0.5,"Strong", IF(ABS(B5)>=0.3,"Moderate", IF(ABS(B5)>=0.1,"Weak", "Not"))))	Uses a rule of thumb like .75, .5. & .3 to determine how strong the relationship is

Since Excel can create the R with a built-in Pearson formula and has the T Distribution also built in, there are just a few additional Excel Formulas you'll want to use as well. And the particular cell/column references pictured need to be adjusted to your spreadsheet.

PEARSON('Data (2)'!$P:$P, 'Data (2)'!C:C)

1. Returns a Person R coefficient between two variables

2. This is the column of your behavior or Engagement Score

3. This is your validation variable

COUNTIFS('Data (2)'!$P:$P,">=" & 0, 'Data (2)'!$C:$C,">=" & 0)

1. Returns the number of rows that meet a criteria

2. Only include rows where the behavior/score is greater than or equal to 0. Serves as a proxy to remove null values, text, and headers from the counts.

3. Only include rows where the validation variable is greater than or equal to 0.

(ABS(B5)*SQRT(B6-2))/(SQRT(1-ABS(B5)^2))

1. ABS returns the "absolute value". Essentially, making a negative into a positive. The Pearson can identify positive and negative relationships (Positive: both go up or down together. Negative: as one goes up, the other goes down and vice versa). At this point, we are just determining the strength, not the direction of the relationship. So converting a -.75 into a .75 is easier to evaluate.

2. This references the Pearson R

3. We need to multiply the Pearson R by the square root of the Pairs (number of records with a Score/behavior and the validation variable) minus the degrees of freedom

4. The absolute value of the Pearson R is squared. That value is subtracted from "1" and is used to divide into our above value. This is our t-test to determine if the Pearson R is significantly different from 0 based on our data.

TDIST(B7, (B6-2), 2)

1. A T Distribution looks very similar to a normal distribution (bell curve) but the former has fatter tail(s). Excel already has this in its system to compare to return a P Value

2. This is out T value from the above formula

3. The number of rows minus our degrees of freedom

4. Using a two-tailed test, which is more conservative and a logical default in most cases. Using a one-tailed test would require knowing the relationship between the variables. A reasonable assumption given an Engagement Score should be positively correlated with things like applying enrolling and staff evaluations.

IF(B8 <0.05, "Yes", "No")

1. Makes a logical evaluation of if a scenario is true and return programmed values based on the results

2. Scenario: Is the P Value less than .05 (a rule of thumb for statistical significance)

3. If true, return "Yes"

4. If not true, return "No"

IF(ABS(B5)>=0.75,"Very Strong",

IF(ABS(B5)>=0.5,"Strong",

IF(ABS(B5)>=0.3,"Moderate",

IF(ABS(B5)>=0.1,"Weak",

"Not")))

1. Makes a logical evaluation of if a scenario is true and return programmed values based on the results

2. Is the absolute value (change negatives into positives) of the Pearson R greater than or equal to .75 (a rule of thumb)

3. If true, return "Very Strong"

4. If not true, calculate another IF statement

5. If not true, return "Not"

For statistical significance, I tend to use .05 (other popular cutoffs are .01 and .001). This is not a perfect evaluation of your relationship between the behavior/score and the validation variable. The number of students in the historical data you're using will affect whether or not you get a "Yes" or "No".

That's why it's important to also assess how strong the relationship is. Another rule of thumb uses the Pearson R value. If it's above .5, it is a strong relationship. Above .3 is a moderate relationship. And above .1 is a weak relationship.

Pearson Rs will range from -1 to 1, so a .65 and -65 are both strong relationships. The .65 indicates that as the new Score goes up, so will the validation variable being used to "test" the new Score. The -.65 shows that as the new Score goes up, the validation variable will go down and vice versa.

Since these are just rules of thumb, you will need to determine what cutoffs make the most sense at your institution and with the available data. Being able to interpret values like "Yes" and "Very Strong" are much easier than evaluating the actual numbers, especially with established cutoffs.

Using Conditional Formatting with these cells also makes it easier to evaluate at a glance. You are essentially heatmapping your results.

Essentially this recreates those IF formulas. If the cell value = "Not", then the cell background becomes red. But as the effect becomes stronger, the colors shift towards dark green. If you are adding a hundred behaviors (or a hundred different versions of the data you do have), it becomes critical to quickly and easily evaluate each behavior.

This comes with the caveat of randomly evaluating hundreds of relationships with statistics may lead you to find random effects that aren't actually significant or helpful. Typically to counter this, more conservative statistics and cutoffs are used. But nothing that properly accounts for this kind of fishing expedition.

Pictured above: Our favorite superhero Quickster pausing to go on a fishing trip in our data lake. The viewer is invited to stay vigilant for the dastardly return of Downstream Consequences

This is definitely a spreadsheet that can lead you down a rabbit hole while trying to perfect the new Score. A few words of caution would be that sometimes "good enough" is best. Spending 5 hours to get 90% of a perfect Score is likely better than spending 50 hours to get 95%.

It is worth pointing out that this process uses historical records to build a Score, which will be applied on new records. Something that perfectly describes historical data is not the goal. In fact, something that rigid and detailed may overfit and have trouble accurately describing new records. Pilot the Score and adjust on the fly as new data comes in. Experience with how the Score is working in the wild and developing ways to improve will be more beneficial than endlessly tinkering with it in preproduction.

If the historical dataset is large enough, additional validation can be done on those historical records to examine how generalizable the rubric is. But again, future records will have another degree of separation from historical records, even those not in the original training data. This becomes clearer as we consider the shifting landscape of higher education - COVID-19 Pandemic, FAFSA Simplification, Enrollment and Search Cliffs, SCOTUS, etc.

When you add new records into this Excel document to evaluate how well the rubric is working on new students, the Score is not going to be as "accurate" as it described the training data. But it is key to have an impactful tool.

This new year of data can be added to the training data to augment the rubric. It can also add a datapoint to a longitudinal study of data trends. Perhaps students are systematically shifting how they engage with the institution. So to accurately capture future records, updating the rubric to lead that change may be helpful in getting more impact. But such extrapolations are a risky change without thorough planning, strategy, and understanding.

Another hurdle for accurately describing student engagement is the simple fact that Slate will never have a complete picture of records. These are essentially just a few snapshots Slate has taken of them. There's missing context in how students engaged with the institution. Engaged also being a keyword. What is the institution doing differently now that's not being captured in some/all of these records? A new form? A new type of event or bigger institutional push to host events? These changes require more than a bit of human thought to accommodate for in this process.

Conclusion

Excel is a powerful and flexible tool for data exploration, Scoring, and validation in higher education. By leveraging Excel's capabilities, you can streamline the Engagement Scoring process, validate results, and gain valuable insights into student engagement.

This chapter used Excel for Engagement Scoring and offered practical tips for maximizing its capabilities. By adopting these strategies, you can enhance your institution's recruitment efforts and drive success across the student lifecycle.

The following chapters will continue building an Engagement Score before exploring the role of Predictive Modeling in higher education as well as providing practical guidance for leveraging these tools to achieve institutional goals.

CHAPTER 4: BONUSES IN ENGAGEMENT SCORING SYSTEMS

As you implement automated Engagement Scoring systems in Slate, it is essential to account for nuances and variations in student behavior. Not all students will have the same opportunities to demonstrate interest, attend events, or engage with the institution in ways that are traditionally tracked. This is where bonuses play a critical role in refining and balancing Engagement Scores. By introducing bonuses, you can ensure that your Engagement Scoring system is fair, accessible, and reflective of student interest, rather than simply rewarding students who have more opportunities to engage.

This chapter explores the rationale behind adding bonuses to Engagement Scores, different types of bonuses, and practical methods for incorporating them into Slate's Scoring systems.

Why Use Bonuses In Engagement Scoring?

Bonuses are not just a way to "sweeten" a student's Engagement Score. They serve a much deeper purpose in ensuring fairness, accessibility, and accuracy in the way student behaviors are evaluated. There are three primary reasons to use bonuses in Engagement Scoring:

Fine-tuning the Score: Adjusting Scores to more accurately reflect genuine student engagement rather than relying strictly on averaged inputs.

Ensuring Accessibility: Compensating for students who may not have the same access to opportunities like campus visits or in-person events.

Addressing Opportunity Gaps: Preventing students from being penalized for missed behaviors due to circumstances beyond their control, such as not needing to submit financial aid forms or missing limited availability events.

Fine-Tuning Engagement Scores

Engagement Scores aggregate behaviors, but not every behavior carries equal weight, and sometimes students who exhibit fewer behaviors may still be highly engaged. For example, attending one event and attending two events can look very different on paper, but in reality, the difference in engagement may be negligible. This is where bonuses come into play as a tool for **fine-tuning**.

Instead of over-complicating formulas or scaling each behavior's contribution, bonuses allow for a simpler approach. Consider a situation where attending one campus event is worth 10 points, and attending two events is worth 20 points.

Someone attending an event may be 10 "points" more engaged than another student who did not attend an event. Is a third student who attended a second event twice as engaged as the first student's event behavior? Perhaps attending an event at all is worth 5 points in the form of a bonus and each individual event is worth 5 points.

Instead of doubling the points automatically for two events, a bonus can help even out the Score and avoid disproportionate rewards for behaviors that don't significantly alter the engagement picture or have a perfectly linear relationship.

You will likely find the difference between increases in engagement will vary between the numbers of behaviors, likely the largest going from 0 to 1. But perhaps students tend to take a Campus Tour and Information Session together. A bonus can be created to account for increases associated with a second visit if that is indicative of another jump in engagement beyond a simple SUM of events. Here are some example rubrics. Which option delivers the most impact, decreases complexity, and reduces the risk of error for you?

Equal-weighted Score, No Bonus	Equal-weighted Score, With Bonuses	Tailored Score, No Bonus
1 Event: 10 points • 10-pt event 2 Events (same day): 20 points • 10-pt event • 10-pt event 2 Events (multiple visits): 20 points • 10-pt event • 10-pt event 2 Events (same day): 30 points • 10-pt event • 10-pt event • 10-pt event 3 Events (multiple visits): 30 points • 10-pt event • 10-pt event • 10-pt event	1 Event: 10 points • 5-pt bonus (any event) • 5-pt event 2 Events (same day): 15 points • 5-pt bonus (any event) • 5-pt event • 5-pt event 2 Events (multiple visits): 25 points • 5-pt bonus (any event) • 10-pt bonus (multiple visits) • 5-pt event • 5-pt event 3 Events (same day): 20 points • 5-pt bonus (any event) • 5-pt event • 5-pt event	1 Event: 10 points • 10-pt 1st event 2 Events (same day): 15 points • 10-pt 1st event • 5-pt 2nd event 2 Events (multiple visits): 15 points • 10-pt 1st event • 5-pt 2nd event 3 Events (same day): 18 points • 10-pt 1st event • 5-pt 2nd event • 3-pt 3rd event 3 Events (multiple visits): 18 points • 10-pt 1st event • 5-pt 2nd event • 3-pt 3rd event

	· 5-pt event
	3 Events (multiple visits):
	30 points
	    · 5-pt bonus (any event)
	    · 10-pt bonus (multiple visits)
	    · 5-pt event
	    · 5-pt event
	    · 5-pt event	

Bonuses offer incredible utility and simplicity, which makes them my preferred option to tailor and augment Scores. They can smooth out Scoring curves, ensuring that high-engagement students who demonstrate a wide range of behaviors receive credit, but those who engage heavily in one area without overloading the system with redundant actions still show accurate interest levels.

Ensuring Accessibility in Engagement Scoring

When designing an Engagement Scoring system, **accessibility** should be an integral part of the conversation. Students come from a wide variety of socioeconomic and geographic backgrounds as well as physio-mental barriers, which can hinder their ability to engage in certain behaviors, such as in-person campus visits or attendance at local events. For example, some students may lack the financial resources to travel to campus for a tour, while international students or students with disabilities may have physical or logistical barriers that prevent them from attending in-person events.

Engagement Scores that heavily favor in-person interactions inadvertently become proxies for factors like financial status or geographic proximity rather than true measures of interest. Bonuses can counteract this effect by rewarding students who are actively engaging with the institution in other ways—such as attending virtual events, sending emails, or interacting with their admission counselors.

Incorporating these kinds of bonuses ensures that students who are genuinely interested in the institution but face accessibility barriers are not penalized in the Scoring process.

This becomes critical if the Engagement Score is used in the evaluation or decision process. If students above a 50-pt cutoff get preferential treatment because of perceived yield likelihood or other assumptions made by attaining a high Engagement Score, then not accounting for these barriers becomes even more of a disservice to the students and institution.

Addressing Opportunity Gaps

Another critical reason for adding bonuses is to **address gaps in opportunities** for students. Some behaviors are only available to specific subsets of students, and it would be unfair to penalize those who do not have access to these opportunities.

A common example is the submission of the FAFSA (Free Application for Federal Student Aid). Submitting the FAFSA is often considered a strong indicator of student interest and intent, and many institutions assign points for it. However, not all students at all institutions need to submit a FAFSA if they are not applying for financial aid. Without a bonus, these students would lose out on valuable points in the Engagement Score for a behavior they will not perform.

Similarly, if Admission Interviews are first-come, first-serve, then you will have a large population who never really had an opportunity to whatever points were associated with that event

Perhaps both of these excluded groups could still act. Non-aid applicants submitting the FAFSA anyways and "engaged" students signing up for interviews earlier than their counterparts who missed the boat. But is this engagement? A good counselor coaching them on how to score some Demonstrated Interest? Either way, there will be a large group left without a reasonable chance to accrue these points, so a bonus can be applied to their Score to at least partially accommodate the deficit.

Types Of Bonuses

There are several strategies for creating bonuses. Some may lend themselves more naturally for the reason a bonus is being applied, but ultimately, the game of match will be a case-by-case situation at your institution. I provide some general use cases just to offer some initial guidance.

Static Bonuses

A **static bonus** is a fixed number of points added to a student's Score. This type of bonus works well to smooth out Scoring discrepancies and fine-tuning Scores. In the example of event points being boosted by flags attending an event at all or visits happening on multiple trips. They help augment other Scoring practices.

This method is simple, computationally efficient, and easy to communicate to staff, but it may lack the flexibility to account for nuanced differences in student behaviors.

If this method is used to replace a missing behavior, the static value should not (usually) fully replace the missed behavior's points. If a student earns 10 points for submitting the FAFSA, but some students do not have to submit it, those students should not receive the full 10 points. That is not a meaningful bonus that adds to our understanding of those students. After review, a different static value like 3 points or 5 points may be determined. But most situations would benefit from a different approach entirely.

Scaling or Reweighting Bonuses

Scaling or reweighting bonuses provide a more dynamic way to adjust Scores. Rather than simply adding a fixed number of points, scaling bonuses adjust the remaining Score based on the points a student has already earned.

For instance, if a student's Score is missing a 10-point behavior (such as submitting the FAFSA), their total remaining Score could be reduced to fill the missed behavior's points. If the rest of their Score is 50 points, dividing 50 by 9 (or 8 if replacing a 20-pt behavior, etc.) and applying the points results in a scaled bonus of 5.56 points, bringing their adjusted Score to 55.56.

This method allows for more granular control over the bonus and maintains the overall integrity of the Engagement Score. You likely do not want to grant the total number of points they could have received for performing a behavior, so boosting the Score with a reflection of their current engagement offers a reasonable accommodation.

This strategy is more computationally intensive and requires more calibration though. This method also implies that the student's current Score out of the possible points is an accurate percentage of the Score and should be approximate the points possibly obtained. Perhaps a student COULD Score 100 points but the practical ceiling that even highly engaged students Score is more like 65 points, then the student should have received something closer to 7.7 (50/6.5). Or perhaps students in the top 75th percentile of the Engagement Score submit the FAFSA, so students in the top 75th percentile should receive all 10 points of the unobtainable behavior.

This is another rabbit hole that is easy to fall down. And gets more and more computationally intensive the further down you go. I have to remind myself frequently of this proverb - "Where moderate effort will suffice, use moderate effort". May it be a salve for your perfectionist tendencies.

Proxy Behavior Bonuses

Another method for addressing missing behaviors is to use proxy behaviors. For example, if a student didn't attend an in-person event but demonstrated strong virtual engagement, they could receive bonus points based on similar online behaviors, such as participating in virtual events, webinars, or direct interactions with admissions counselors.

Proxy behaviors allow institutions to offer students alternative ways to demonstrate engagement without being penalized for missed opportunities. This type of bonus is particularly effective in scenarios where different engagement channels (online vs. in-person) are available to students.

Local Student (23 Pts)	Out of State Student with Financial Barriers (22 Pts)	Out of State Student visiting many colleges (21 Pts)
2 Events: 20 Pts 1 Portal Logins: 1 Pts 1 Email Sent: 2 Pts	10 Portal Logins: 13 Pts • 3-pt bonus (No events, >= 3 logins) • 10-pt score (1 Pt per login) 3 Email Sent: 9 Pts • 3-pt bonus (No events, >= 3 emails) • 6-pt score (2 Pts per email)	1 Events: 10 Pts 5 Portal Logins: 5 Pts 3 Email Sent: 6 Pts

This will require conversation and analysis around what the appropriate behaviors and amount of points are to supplement the missed behavior. But this can help offset the potentially higher Scores students receive by simply being able to financially visit more colleges in the search process. Or bridge the point gap for those who can't attend due to other barriers. Similarly, it can be used to offset other advantages/behaviors students who receive more college guidance may know to do.

A filter can also be used to grant behaviors specifically to the students with these barriers, but that requires a very extensive and comprehensive understanding of your populations. This is not realistic or advisable in most scenarios, but depending on what the behaviors, barriers, and bonuses are, points can be more mindfully applied to students than the broader population that may benefit despite not facing those barriers.

Conclusion

Bonuses can be a critical component of sophisticated Engagement Scoring systems. They allow institutions to fine-tune Scores, ensure equitable access, and account for opportunity gaps among different student populations. Whether applying static, scaling, or proxy behavior bonuses, institutions can create more accurate, fair, and useful Engagement Scores that truly reflect student interest. This is especially true when the discourse is so heavily centered on behaviors like submitting the FAFSA or attending an event on campus. These are both usually strong indicators, but they do have limitations.

By embracing bonuses as part of Engagement Scoring, you can better support recruitment and admissions strategies while promoting fairness and inclusivity across the student pool.

CHAPTER 5: AUTOMATING AND OPTIMIZING ENGAGEMENT SCORES

An Engagement Score is a valuable thing. If it withers on the vine, then the time, resources, and passion that went into creating it is lost, and the morale of staff who built it will sour. While I like to build my Scoring rubric with a combination of staff collaboration and historical data in Excel, it is critical that the Score is updated, easy to use, and strategically implemented.

This chapter provides an in-depth guide to building and automating Engagement Scoring systems in Slate, focusing on query construction, automating procedures, and making the Score itself easy and intuitive to use.

Queries

Automating Engagement Scoring in Slate requires building

Queries that aggregate data points and apply Scoring rubrics to student behaviors. These Queries then update automatically on your schedule as well as any additional batch updates as needed such as admission committees or large events. This provides admission teams with current insights into student engagement. Later, you will use translation codes to create intuitive and time-specific Score bands that use your current data.

The first step in automating Engagement Scoring is constructing queries that capture the key behaviors indicative of student interest. These behaviors might include event attendance, email interactions, portal logins, application progress, etc. By creating a query that tracks these interactions, you can calculate a comprehensive Engagement Score for each student. Queries will be needed to build your Scoring rubric, calculating live student Scores, and building any required bonuses.

While Configurable Joins has been live since 2021, many institutions have yet to meaningfully switch to them. And even fewer are leveraging them in powerful ways. Even if you haven't tackled them yet, Engagement Scoring will be an excellent field to learn on. And the feature engineering process (and chapter) of Predictive Modeling will get you across the finish line. You'll go pro in no time. And I think I have exhausted the football metaphors (for now).

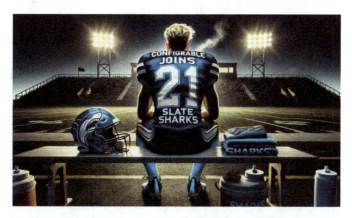

Much like this book is not a statistics textbook, it's also not a Configurable Joins 101 guide. There are wonderful resources in the community and by Partners that will teach you a lot about starting and using CJs. This book will show several screenshots though and walk through the logic.

I like to think of Configurable Joins as a drag and drop interface for SQL. It's a no-code/low-code way to connect different data tables, aggregate behaviors, and engineer features. The vision for my next book is Adaptive Enrollment Management. While the third act of this book applies the AEM lens to using Scoring and Modeling, there are a lot of really fun CJs you will build with a full AEM implementation.

As a general recommendation, create nested subquery exports to clearly define each point of the filters and formulas. This makes understanding the factors easier and updates faster.

Whether you only update once a year or a different staff ends up updating the query, this at-a-glance spelling out will help whoever is working with the query in the future (or even troubleshooting). I typically do the same with Excel and my other work.

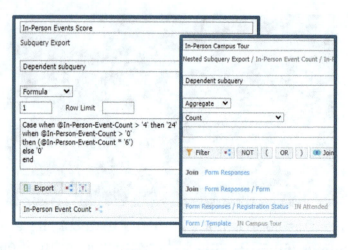

This process may cause you to recreate a few exports as you find you need everything to be nested one layer deeper to put the final touches on the export with a Formula, Concatenation, or Translation code.

This becomes especially true when you get into complicated subqueries. When dealing with time-anchored behaviors (e.g. behaviors happening before the application deadline or that happen in a narrow window after Decisions/Transfer Evaluation/Financial Aid Award is received), this can become even more troublesome but are more in the domain of feature engineering with Predictive Modeling. Most important of all is clearly building your reports. With the different slicing of data, increased number of staff in the report and likely longer use, unclear report building can incapacitate a project.

When I first started building the reports to project Net Tuition Revenue with incorporated nudges (e.g. what is the NTR if 20% of students attend Admitted Student Day), I repeatedly rebuilt this export which had several nested exports, going 7 layers deep.

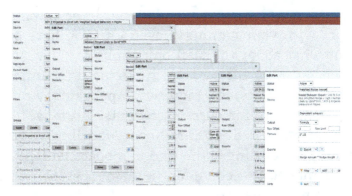

And don't even get me started on the number of times I rebuilt the required exports and filters to create the emails for my Course Insights Engine. That took the outstanding courses for the student, what was being offered, and success indicators to not only recommend classes for students to register for, but also flagged the courses they were more likely to be successful in. Well, maybe. As I write this, AEM and that tool are both books I'd like to write.

Another STRONG recommendation for Scoring and Modeling is to create Slate Fields for your behavior. While you may be able to run these calculations in a query, depending on the number of exports, the size of your population(s), factors like bonus, frequency of the automated updates, and other considerations, dedicated field will not only make life much easier, they will make troubleshooting a much better experience.

While you may run the query for all relevant records, having static fields does allow you to compare the field's existing value with the current math for needed updates. Not to mention the need to replicate rubric changes wherever you need to do these calculations.

Engagement Scores can be something of a gateway tool, so

the flashing marquee recommendation is to be extremely clear and exact with your naming convention. You have one Score now, but what about the MarComm subscore that aggregates a few behaviors. Or the separate rubric used for International students? Or rubrics for Inquiries, Applicants, Admits, etc. The separate Score for current students? Alumnae? Or fields for Application Modeling? Enrollment Modeling? Retention or Philanthropy Modeling? And those models will likely need additional models to account for the differences in predictors for your different populations.

That is all to say, don't name your field "Event Attendance" and call it a day.

Automation

To ensure that Engagement Scores remain current, you can leverage Slate's automation features to schedule regular updates. By automating Score calculations, your team will focus on interpreting the data and making informed decisions, rather than manually updating Scores.

1. **Schedule Query Runs**: Use Slate's Schedule Export to

automate query execution at regular intervals. This ensures that Engagement Scores are updated in real time, reflecting the latest student interactions.

a. Note that the path needs "../incoming/" to place the query results in the "Incoming" folder which is where the Source Format will need them to be to pick it up and import it.

b. Set up an email to receive notification for at least Failures and late deliveries.

c. Schedule the more intensive queries for slower days/times if possible. If there are multiple queries that need to run, staggering the windows will be error-proof that over trying to ingest them in the appropriate order in the same window.

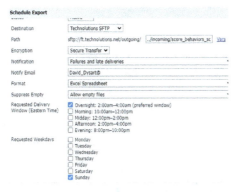

2. **Automate Data Imports**: Automate the import of data with a Source Format

a. There are a few notes on the General Tab -

i. Set Status to Active

ii. Give it a descriptive Name

iii. Remap As Of to capture the earliest file and set Remap Active to Active

iv. Set to Unsafe so current Applicants

can have fields updated (even if you think you set your new fields to Unsafe. No one wants to spend 3 hours troubleshooting the Score just to find out in-person events weren't updating because they were Safe)

v.　　　　Set Update Only

vi.　　　　　Set Notifications to at least email relevant staff on Failures

vii.　　　　Adjust other settings as needed.

b. Under the Format Definition Tab, this code in the XML box tells Slate that the first row in your file is the Header with Column Names

i.　　　　　<layout type="convert" h="1" />

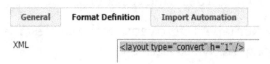

c. The last important piece to update is in the

Import Automation Tab. You must add the name specified in the Query's Scheduled Export. This tells Slate what file to pick up and ingest. This picture example uses an asterisk wildcard to look for the file name and any additional text where the "*" is at. This is important if you are adding a timestamp.

c. If you have multiple Scheduled Exports that may be picked up, you will need to revise your naming convention. "score_behaviors_score*.xlsx" would pick up all three of these files:

  i. score_behaviors_score.xlsx

  ii. score_behaviors_score_09082024.xlsx

  iii. Score_behaviors_score_pt2_bonuses. xlsx

Some of the automation and calculations can be offloaded to Rules. In my experience, I prefer running everything through the Query and Source Format process. But you can experiment with including Rules into your process to make your own decision. Ultimately, the processes and build are similar.

Data Transformation And Integration

In the earlier chapter on creating a Scoring rubric, you created a Score where 100 points was the maximum possible Score. And truly, I stand by that recommendation generally. It helps create a balanced Score as it provides an architecture and enforced scarcity. You have no option other than to be mindful and judicious with the behaviors and rubric.

The other side of that coin is it always provides a point of reference for interpreting the Score of an individual or group. Given the encompassing nature of different forms of engagement and progressive nature of the recruitment cycle. Students simply aren't going to score a 100.

Scoring an 85 isn't a B. A student Scoring 20 at the beginning of the cycle might be one of the highest Scores. By the time of Decision Release, maybe that 20 is on the lower side. And while it may be easier to fit behaviors into a 100-pt score, your staff may be socialized to a 1-5, A-F, or 1-10.

A user-friendly framework comes with transforming the Engagement Score with a Translation Code.

Edit Translation Code		Edit Translation Code	
Key	sample_di_score	Key	sample_di_score
Type	Real Number (Inclusive Range of Values)	Type	Real Number (Inclusive Range of Values)
Status	Active	Status	Active
Minimum Value	-Notes	Minimum Value	19.501
Maximum Value		Maximum Value	33.199
Export Value	1-5 (Staff Evaluation)	Export Value	2
Export Value 2	Low, Medium, High	Export Value 2	Low
Export Value 3	Quintile	Export Value 3	4th
Export Value 4	Percentile (and used to calculate Quentile)	Export Value 4	40%
Export Value 5		Export Value 5	

Translation Codes give several options. Any Score between 10 and 30 can become one of the following in a query, Dashboard, Report, Portal, Voyager, or as a Merge Field.

The first Export Value pictured is where their Score lands on a 1-5 scale. We'll detail how to set this Score band shortly.

Export Value 2 uses a description like "Low", "Medium", and "High". The third and fourth Export Values are more descriptive of the data in your institution/subgroups.

The Translation Code will not inherently scale to your instance's data (and I would not recommend doing it internally in Slate). Translation Codes can be created and updated with an Excel file through Upload Dataset.

You may need to activate the Source Format from the Library. If you were not using this process to create and update Translation Code values, this may truly unlock the tool at your institution. There are so many ways Translation Codes can transform your processes, and being able to batch them through Excel makes it so much faster and easier to manage than manually interacting with Slate's user interface.

Source Format Library

	transla	
Name	**Format**	**Status**
Translation Code Import	Excel	Added

After activating the Source Format, you will need to download the current list/template spreadsheet from your Standard Query Library.

Standard Query Library

Selecting a query from the list below will run

Name

Current Translation Code List

You do not need to upload all values every time to upload the spreadsheet. Just the ones you want to update or create. If you are updating a value, you will need the ID from the file, otherwise, Slate will create a new key instead of updating what you wanted to update. Not the funnest time.

All Standard Queries

Current Translation Code List							Show SQL	Refresh Results	Download to Excel		
ID	Active	Default	Key	Type	minValue	maxValue	Export	Export2	Export3	Export4	Export5

What I would recommend is building a query with your relevant group of students that you need behavior data on. Export this data and add it as a tab in your Translation Code Upload Excel file.

The Score bands are created by referencing the Quintiles in your Translation Code Uploads tab, making the bands specific to your current pool of students you just downloaded. The Translation Codes must be the left-most tab in your file when uploading to Slate's Upload Dataset tool.

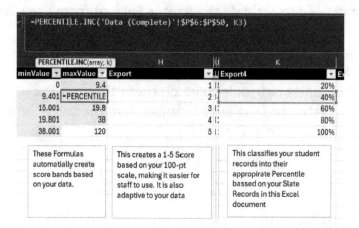

`=PERCENTILE.INC('Data (Complete)'!$P$6:$P$50, K3)`

PERCENTILE.INC(array, k)		H			K	
minValue	maxValue	Export		Export4		E>
0	9.4		1		20%	
9.401	=PERCENTILE		2		40%	
15.001	19.8		3		60%	
19.801	38		4		80%	
38.001	120		5		100%	

These Formulas automatially create score bands based on your data.	This creates a 1-5 Score based on your 100-pt scale, making it easier for staff to use. It is also adaptive to your data	This classifies your student records into their appropirate Percentile bassed on your Slate Records in this Excel document

When you want to refresh your Translation Code bands, you can either use the live sync function with your Query or Download the updated data from Slate and simply upload the file again since the formulas are all live, making this a quick process that can be completed as often as needed through the cycle.

So not only does the Translation Code provide context to what a specific Score means, it is specific to the current time in the cycle.

Later chapters will cover several uses for this Score, but I want to make one more recommendation that makes the Score itself more utilizable on a day-to-day basis.

Embedding the Score (and Predictive Modeling values) into a Dashboard on the Slate Record provides additional context for the student as people interact with them. This example comes from a wonderful former colleague - Paloma Barragan who was redesigning the Dashboard at the time and integrated the new Scores while doing it.

Depending on which step of the funnel the student was in, it flipped between predictive models - Likelihood to Apply and Likelihood to Enroll. It also uses the raw Engagement Score as well as translating it to 5 stars.

Min Value	Max Value	Export Value
New Code		
0	9.5	1
09.501	13.199	2
13.2	21.799	3
21.8	35.4	4
35.401	120	5

Dysart, Dahveed

Dashboard	Timeline	2022 RD Decided	Profile	Materials	Additional Information	Committed	Operation

Dashboard

Chosen Name	Staff Assigned	Likelihood to Enroll	DI Score
Dahveed	David Dysart	57%	★★★☆☆ 14/100

Student Type	Planned Entry Year	Texting Okay?	Last Email Opened:
First Year	FA 2022	No	11/11/2021
			Last Login: 9/1/2021

Events Registered: 1   Attended: 1
▶ See event details.

Conclusion

Automating Engagement Scores gives you a powerful tool for optimizing recruitment and admissions strategies. By building queries that aggregate data points and applying Scoring logic, you can create dynamic Scoring models that provide valuable insights into student engagement.

With Slate automating the update process (with additional manual updates easy to do in Batch Updates), the Score is always an up-to-date reflection of the student's engagement with extremely low maintenance. And the quick process to update Translation Codes makes the context of the Score also timely and relevant.

As the lights dim on Act I, the bright promise of Act II will explore the role of Predictive Modeling in higher education.

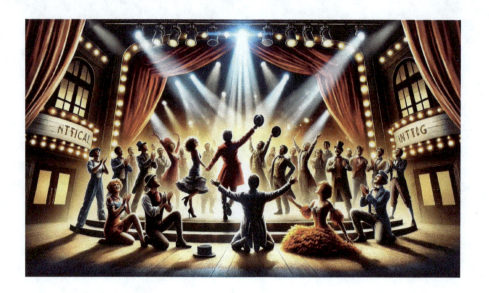

ACT II: PREDICTIVE MODELING

How did your office like automated Scoring in Slate? Did they throw you a party? I bet they did. It's weird though. I didn't get my invite.

It's okay.

There will be another party once you implement application and enrollment Modeling! Or dropout and philanthropy Modeling for my friends just downstream the student lifecycle a bit.

I do love Engagement Scoring though. It's a wonderful tool that allows you to better understand your students, their engagement, and their affinity with your institution. In Act III of this book, you'll learn several ways to use it not only in your day-to-day work but also in your broader strategy and resource allocation.

Another thing I love about Engagement Scoring is that it is an excellent primer for building and using Predictive Modeling. In many ways, Predictive Modeling is the next natural step and evolution of Engagement Scoring.

This Act will serve as a more in-depth primer for the Modeling (but don't worry, I'm not talking Jules Verne-level of depths. Though I suppose you can call me Captain Nemo if you'd like). It is by no means a statistics textbook. I merely pondered what I would have wanted as a quickstart guide doing Predictive Modeling.

You do not need to be a statistician or Slate wizard to move your institution forward. There are likely resources, staff, and faculty that can help transform prospective students into graduates with a bit of Slate magic.

That said, Engagement Scoring does have its own pros. It is a good indicator with less maintenance, time, and expertise to build than a full predictive model. It can also ingest behaviors from a broader portion of the funnel/time (early app, decision stage, yield stage, etc.) and still display a relevant Score within the context of the applicant pool.

The benefits of Predictive Modeling can be magnified though, especially if your institution has many stealth applicants who do enroll even though they have low engagement. A predictive model is also more "finetuned" than the Score, especially when focused on a particular part of the funnel. And while an

Engagement Score can be validated and correlated to a behavior like applying and enrolling, if you want to understand, project, and be proactive, then Predictive Modeling is the tool for the job.

Predictive Modeling particularly shines when understanding the behavioral and ecospherical data associated with applying and enrolling - and how to leverage that prescriptively to improve the student and institutional outcomes.

But look at me getting ahead of myself. Let's learn to walk before we run. While this next part is not a statistics textbook, there's still plenty for me to convey to you with the building, automation, and use of Predictive Modeling for your institution.

How about we go for that walk?

Emerging from the shadow of Engagement Scoring, Predictive Modeling has proven to be a powerful tool for meeting goals, enhancing institutional strategies, and improving student outcomes. Modeling provides valuable insights that inform strategic decision-making across various aspects of higher education. We'll explore how it works, what it is, and some benefits with a focus on applications within Slate.

Predictive Modeling is a statistical technique that uses historical data to make predictions about future events or behaviors. By identifying patterns and relationships within the data, Models can forecast a wide range of outcomes, from student application likelihood to enrollment probability and retention rates. In the context of higher education, Predictive Modeling empowers institutions to make data-driven decisions that enhance recruitment efforts, improve student retention, and support overall student success.

In today's data-rich environment, higher education institutions are increasingly turning to Predictive Modeling to gain an edge. They allow you to tailor your recruitment strategies more effectively. Predictive Models help plan and meet goals, identify high-impact prospects and areas, and optimize outreach efforts to increase yield rates.

Predictive Models can inform decisions about resource allocation, such as staffing needs, financial aid distribution, and program development. By anticipating future trends and demands, institutions can optimize their operations and enhance the student experience.

How Predictive Modeling Works

Predictive Modeling involves several key steps, including data collection, data checking and cleaning, model development, validation, and deployment (repeat, always repeat). The process begins with the collection of historical data, which serves as the foundation for building predictive models. Data is then analyzed to identify patterns and relationships that can inform predictions about future behaviors.

Data Collection: Historical data is collected from various sources, including student information systems, Slate , 3rd-party data, and other data systems. This data includes information about student demographics, interactions, academic performance, population trends, and engagement behaviors. Feature engineering, building new datapoints based on multiples pieces of data may increase model performance

Data Checking and Cleaning: Different models and machine learning algorithms have different prerequisites and assumptions that must be checked and met. Additional work cleaning, screening, and working with the data will be needed.

Model Development: Statistical techniques are used to develop predictive models that identify patterns and relationships within the data. Models are trained using historical data to make predictions about future outcomes. New types of data (virtual events), changes in the students and environmental context, and other limitations can make historical data difficult to correctly predict behaviors.

Validation: Models are validated to ensure their accuracy, reliability, and not biased. This involves testing the model's predictions against actual outcomes and making necessary adjustments to improve performance. In a simple process, this can include using about 75% of your data to build the model and 25% to validate it. Other methods typically require more advanced techniques.

Deployment: Once validated, predictive models are deployed to generate forecasts and inform decision-making. Models can be integrated into existing systems, such as Slate, to provide real-time insights and support strategic planning.

Choosing A Predictive Model

Predictive Modeling relies on a variety of statistical methods to identify patterns and relationships within data and generate forecasts. While this book focuses on Binary Logistic Regression, there are many paths you can take, so we'll quickly detour to cover some of the options.

Binary Logistic Regression

Binary Outcomes: Logistic regression is used to model binary outcomes, where the dependent variable has two possible values (e.g., apply or not apply, enroll or not enroll).

Logit Function: Logistic regression uses a logit function to model the probability of the outcome variable. The logit function transforms the probability into a continuous scale, allowing for linear relationships between the predictor variables and the outcome.

Odds Ratios: Logistic regression estimates the odds ratios for each predictor variable, indicating the likelihood of the outcome occurring for a given value of the predictor variable. Odds ratios provide insights into the relative importance of different factors in predicting outcomes.

Interpreting Coefficients: The coefficients in a logistic regression model represent the change in the log-odds of the outcome for a one-unit increase in the predictor variable.

Positive coefficients indicate an increased likelihood of the outcome, while negative coefficients indicate the opposite. For example, if the Campus Visit predictor has an unstandardized regression coefficient of 2, one additional event increases the log odds by 2. If the coefficient is -3, then one additional event decreases the log odds by 3.

Predictive models and machine learning algorithms lay on a spectrum of replicability. Binary logistic regression is relatively easy to replicate and automate in Slate. You can also quickly understand how important the features are at a glance and make proactive and prescriptive changes to strategy in real time and update projections based on these hypothetical changes in behaviors and engagements. Models like this become essentially a Prescriptive Assistant for you. They help and augment your team, work, and goals.

A deep neural network not so much. While interpretable models provide a lot of strategic flexibility, black box or even just more obtusely explainable machine learning models like Decision Trees cannot be so seamlessly integrated into Slate and business processes. These powerful tools require additional infrastructure and technical debt that a simpler solution like binary logistic regression can offer within existing systems.

That is not to degrade or devalue those tools. They are advanced and impactful tools. And if you have the time, resources, and staffing to wrap around them, they could still be wonderful avenues to venture down. And the ability to have autonomous algorithms will become too valuable not to utilize, likely soon. This book just is not as applicable to those solutions and approaches.

In addition to binary logistic regression, several other statistical methods are commonly used in Predictive Modeling. These methods provide additional tools for analyzing data and generating forecasts. A brief description of a couple alternatives -

Linear Regression is used to model relationships between continuous variables. It is used to predict outcomes that are not binary, such as student GPA or test scores.

Decision Trees are a non-parametric method used to model complex relationships between variables. They provide a visual representation of decision rules and are useful for identifying important predictors of outcomes.

Random Forests are an ensemble method that combines multiple decision trees to improve prediction accuracy. They are used to model complex relationships and reduce overfitting.

Support Vector Machines (SVMs) are a supervised learning method used to classify data and identify patterns. They are used to model complex relationships and improve prediction accuracy.

Neural Networks are a machine learning method used to model complex relationships between variables. They are particularly useful for Modeling non-linear relationships and large data sets.

Applying Predictive Modeling In Slate Crm

Slate will be an important reservoir of historical data to build your model. And provided you use a Modeling technique that can be replicated in Slate's Formula Exports (a light version of SQL), Slate can automatically apply the model similar to the Engagement Score process earlier in the book. By leveraging Slate's capabilities, you can apply Predictive Modeling to enhance recruitment, retention, and student success efforts. Alternatively, the final Scores/values can be sent to Slate to be used, though it would be in a less impactful series of tools as some of the techniques and strategies discussed in Act III require behavior values.

This is one reason why I prefer Binary Logistic Regression. It's a great utility play - projecting your incoming class, programmable into Slate, modifiable with anticipated actions/ nudges, comparison for interventions, and benchmark for outreach and programming.

The model's simplicity means that Slate can run your entire process after the model itself is built in a system like SPSS or R. With the model math replicated in Slate, the calculations are done in-system and automatically. Alternatives and nudges are relatively easy to apply, showing how outcomes may change if different students are admitted, or if some percent of students display behaviors like attending an Admitted Student Day next month.

This can move time and labor-intensive work into Slate, available one Refresh away.

Conclusion

Predictive Modeling is a powerful tool for enhancing your institutional strategies and improving student outcomes. By leveraging historical data to forecast future behaviors, Models provide valuable insights that inform strategic decision-making across various domains.

We've introduced the concept of Predictive Modeling and provided an overview of the statistical methods used in the process. By applying Predictive Modeling in Slate, institutions can enhance recruitment, retention, and student success efforts, driving success across the student lifecycle.

This Act will explore the technical details of implementing predictive models in Slate, providing practical guidance for leveraging these tools to achieve institutional goals.

CHAPTER 6: BUILDING PREDICTIVE MODELS

Now that we know more about Predictive Models, our next step is to build one so you can start integrating it into Slate and your processes. This chapter provides some information and guidance on the steps, using statistical software, and explores key concepts in Predictive Modeling.

Developing Predictive Models

Building Predictive Models involves a series of systematic steps, from selecting and building the right data to validating the model and integrating it into institutional processes. The below guide will help to develop effective Models. This brief primer though is not meant to be a replacement for a statistics textbook or class.

Step 1: Data Selection and Preparation

The foundation of any predictive model is high-quality data. Selecting and preparing the right data is crucial for building accurate and reliable Models. When building binary logistic regression models, you'll need to follow a few key steps for data screening, assumptions, and checks to ensure the models are robust:

1. Data Screening

- **Missing Data**: Check for missing values in your dataset and decide how to handle them. Options include removing rows with missing data or imputing values. This could be with an average, imputational regression, among other options. We'll discuss this more in the Data chapter.

- **Outliers**: Identify outliers in continuous variables. Outliers can skew your model's results. You may need to remove or transform them if they're unduly influencing your model. If you will be replicating the math in Slate, any transformations will need to be replicated there as well. You will also need to check/ handle multivariate outliers with something like Mahalanobis distance.

- **Data Types**: Ensure that categorical variables are coded as such (e.g., binary or dummy variables), and continuous variables are appropriately formatted.

2. Multicollinearity

- **Variance Inflation Factor (VIF)**: Use VIF to check if any of the predictor variables are highly correlated with one another. High multicollinearity can distort the significance of predictors. A VIF value above 5 (or sometimes 10) indicates multicollinearity.

- **Correlations**: Generate a correlation matrix to examine relationships between predictors. High correlations suggest redundancy, which may impact the model's performance.

3. Linearity of the Logit

- **Continuous Predictors**: Logistic regression assumes a linear relationship between the logit (the natural log of the odds of the dependent variable) and the continuous independent variables. You can check this by plotting each predictor against the logit and looking for linearity.

- **Transformations**: If linearity is violated, consider transforming variables (e.g., logarithmic transformation) or adding polynomial terms to capture non-linear relationships. Again, transformations will have to be replicated in Slate to unlock the full Adaptive Enrollment Management suite of strategies. Transformed variables will also be harder to explain to your constituents.

4. Independence of Errors

- Ensure that observations are independent of each other. This is particularly relevant when dealing with time-series data or grouped data where there may be correlation between observations.

- If your data has grouped structures (e.g., students from the same high school), consider using mixed models or hierarchical logistic regression to account for this.

5. Adequate Sample Size

- Logistic regression requires a minimum number of cases for reliable results. As a general rule of thumb, you should have at least 10 events (successes or failures) per predictor variable. This helps avoid overfitting and ensures reliable parameter estimates. I've also seen that recommendation go to 50 events per predictor. And to clarify, if you are breaking a predictor into multiple variables, then we are reference the number of variables, not "predictors".

6. Balancing Classes

- **Imbalanced Data**: If one outcome is much more common than the other (e.g., far more non-applicants than applicants as is likely), your model might struggle to predict the rarer event. Consider oversampling the minority class, undersampling the majority class, or using techniques like SMOTE (Synthetic Minority Over-sampling Technique). This could easily become an issue with a broad funnel and lower application and enrolling rates.

7. Goodness-of-Fit

- **Hosmer-Lemeshow Test**: This test assesses the goodness of fit for your model. A significant result suggests a poor fit, so you may need to adjust your model or variables if the test flags issues. A large sample may steer this into implying a poor fit.

- **Pseudo-R^2 (Nagelkerke, Cox & Snell)**: While traditional R^2 doesn't apply to logistic regression, pseudo-R^2 values can give a sense of the model's explanatory power.

8. Model Diagnostics

- **Residual Analysis**: Examine deviance and Pearson residuals to identify any problematic observations or potential issues with model specification.

- **Influential Observations**: Use metrics like Cook's distance to detect observations that have a large impact on model estimates. Influential observations may need special attention.

9. Interaction Terms

- Consider testing for interaction effects between variables. Sometimes, the relationship between a predictor and the outcome depends on the value of another predictor. While most students may enroll when they have a large level of engagement, a stealth applicant may enroll with low engagement, so factoring that interaction may help improve your model.

10. Validation

- **Cross-Validation**: Perform k-fold cross-validation or use a holdout dataset to check how well your model generalizes to unseen data.

- **Calibration**: Check how well the predicted probabilities align with actual outcomes (calibration plot), ensuring your model is making realistic predictions.

Following these steps will help ensure that your binary logistic regression models are robust and reliable for predicting prospect applications and enrollments.

In Elaboratione (Latin for "In Elaboration" where I will expand and offer some additional guidance)

On the topic of Hosmer

As a note, when a model is built at scale, it may begin stretching some of the statistical assumptions of such a rigid analysis as Binary Logistic Regression. I do lay awake at night sometimes wondering if Hosmer likes doughnuts as much as his 's'-less counterpart. That may indicate how serious I take Hosmer, especially for larger institutions since the number of students gets so high.

Terminus: In Elaboratione (Latin for "End: In Elaboration")

Let's take a closer look at next steps -

1. **Identify Key Data Sources**: Begin by identifying the key data sources needed for Predictive Modeling. This includes student demographics, academic performance, engagement behaviors, and historical enrollment data. A highlight of Slate is its ability to easily collect live data and import data from other systems and vendors.

2. **Export Data from Slate**: Use Slate Queries to extract the relevant data. Configurable Joins provides much greater control, flexibility, and power to create impactful variables for your model. You will likely need to code variables in several ways to examine

their roles in the model - Yes/No attended an event flag, a sum of the number of events attended, orbital behaviors around Moments that Matter, etc.

3. **Clean and Prepare Data**: Once exported, clean the data to ensure accuracy and consistency. This involves removing duplicates, handling missing values, and standardizing data formats. Tools like Excel or statistical software such as SPSS or R can be used for this purpose. This also requires conversations around practices like concluding events and mapping or entering data from incoming sources.

4. **Feature Engineering**: Create new features or variables that might improve the model's predictive power. This could include interactions between variables or transformations of existing data (e.g., converting continuous variables into categorical ones). We'll discuss this more in the Feature Engineering chapter.

Step 2: Selecting a Modeling Approach

Choosing the right statistical method is essential for building an effective Predictive Model. The choice of Model depends on the nature of the data, the specific outcomes you are trying to predict, and how you will be using it.

1. **Choose a Statistical Method**: Common statistical methods used in Predictive Modeling include binary logistic regression, decision trees, and random forests.

Binary logistic regression is often preferred for predicting binary outcomes (e.g., whether a student will enroll or not). It's also what we will cover in this book.

2. **Set Up the Model in Statistical Software**: Use statistical software like SPSS or R to set up the Model. Import the cleaned and prepared data into systems and apply the model in Slate or another system.

Pro Tip: While working in SPSS, "Paste"-ing the action in the user interface creates the code in the syntax file (which can also be hand-coded or copy/pasted). Running Syntax files can speed up the process, reduce errors, and increase consistency. It can also provide a notated log of the process being performed.

3.   **Define the Outcome Variable**: Clearly define the outcome variable you are trying to predict. For example, in a model predicting enrollment likelihood, the outcome variable would be binary (enroll/not enroll). Some noise can be introduced with coding a student taking a gap year or some similar outcome where your student may look more like one outcome but technically coded as the other depending on the use.

4.   **Select Predictor Variables**: Choose predictor variables based on their potential impact on the outcome. These could include academic metrics, engagement behaviors, demographic information, etc.

Step 3: Model Development and Training

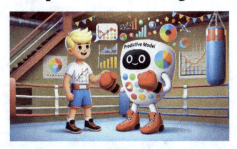

Developing and training the Model involves using the chosen statistical method to identify patterns and relationships within the data.

1. **Split the Data into Training and Testing Sets**: Divide the data into a training set and a testing set. The training set is used to develop the Model, while the testing set is used to evaluate its performance.

2. **Train the Model**: Use the training set to develop the Model. The statistical software will use the data to estimate the parameters of the Model and identify the most important predictors.

3. **Evaluate Model Performance**: Assess the model's performance using metrics such as accuracy, precision, recall, and the area under the receiver operating characteristic (ROC) curve. This evaluation helps determine how well the Model predicts the outcome variable.

4. **Refine the Model**: Based on the evaluation results, refine the Model by adjusting parameters, adding or removing variables, and exploring different Modeling techniques to improve accuracy and reliability.

Step 4: Model Validation and Testing

Validation is a critical step in ensuring the model's accuracy and generalizability to new data.

1. **Validate the Model Using the Testing Set**: Apply the model to the testing set and compare the predicted outcomes to the actual outcomes. This helps assess the model's predictive power and identify any areas for improvement.

2. **Cross-Validation**: Perform cross-validation by dividing the data into multiple subsets and training the Model on different combinations of these subsets. This helps ensure that the Model is robust and not overly fitted to a particular data set.

3. **Assess Model Stability**: Check the stability of the model over time and across different student cohorts. This involves evaluating whether the model performs consistently across various groups and time periods.

Key Concepts in Predictive Modeling

To effectively develop and apply predictive models, it is essential to understand key concepts such as logistic regression, odds ratios, and model fit. This section provides a deeper dive into these concepts, offering the technical knowledge needed for successful Predictive Modeling.

Logistic Regression

Logistic regression is a widely used statistical method for predicting binary outcomes. It models the relationship between one or more predictor variables and a binary dependent variable, such as whether a student will enroll or not.

1. **Binary Outcomes**: Logistic regression is used when the outcome variable is binary, meaning it has two possible values. This makes it suitable for predicting outcomes such as application likelihood, enrollment probability, or retention.

2. **Logit Function**: Logistic regression uses a logit function to model the probability of the outcome variable. The logit function transforms the probability into a continuous scale, allowing for linear relationships between the predictor variables and the outcome.

3. **Odds Ratios**: Logistic regression estimates odds ratios for each predictor variable, which indicate the likelihood of the outcome occurring for a given value of the predictor variable. Odds ratios provide insights into the relative importance of different factors in predicting outcomes.

4. **Interpreting the Model**: The coefficients in a logistic regression model represent the change in the log-odds of the outcome for a one-unit increase in the predictor variable. Positive coefficients indicate an increased likelihood of the outcome, while negative coefficients indicate the opposite. For example, if the Campus Visit predictor has an unstandardized regression coefficient of 2, one additional event increases the log odds by 2. If the coefficient is -3, then one additional event decreases the log odds by 3. Transforming your results into an odds ratio or a 0-100% can make interpreting

and explaining your Model easier.

Conclusion

Building Predictive Models involves a systematic process of data selection, model development, validation, and integration into institutional processes.

This chapter has provided a guide to developing predictive models and explored key concepts in Predictive Modeling. By adopting these strategies, you can drive success across the student lifecycle and achieve their goals.

The following chapters will provide more guidance around data and your predictors before we begin leveraging Predictive Models to achieve student and institutional success and goals.

CHAPTER 7: TRAINING DATA
PART 1 - GETTING STARTED

Predictive Modeling in higher education hinges on the careful consideration of your training data. We'll discuss a handful in this chapter to get you out the door and on your way to explore essential elements like data and variable selection, emphasizing the balance between statistical rigor and contextual understanding.

We'll discuss how overfitting can undermine predictive accuracy and highlight techniques to select the most impactful variables, especially in context around your institution, students, and external factors happening in the orbit of college-going decisions. Additionally, we'll address the challenges of missing data and provide strategies to ensure your models effectively capture relevant patterns and make reliable future predictions.

Variable Selection

As a piece of wisdom from your friendly neighborhood Slater. The more times models are run and the more variables are added, the more likely it is to stumble upon random effects and correlations that won't be valuable to use in the future. A similar principle in statistics is when using multivariate analysis, to adjust tests to be more conservative in finding significant results and that's just a handful of tests. If a model is run 100 times with different variables, nothing is adjusting for those random effects. Be mindful and don't just go fishing for factors. After all, a p value of .05 (a standard rule of thumb) indicates that even if there is no relationship, if you ran your test 100 times, you'd still expect to get results like this 5 times. How many ways did you try to put together the puzzle that is your model(s)?

All of that requires data to begin with. Literature, observations, and correlated variables may help start you down the selection process.

Univariate Analysis: Check correlations between possible predictors and the outcome for initial insight, but complement this with more robust checks.

Use p-values: For each variable, test the significance of its relationship with the outcome (e.g., using chi-square tests for categorical variables or t-tests for continuous variables). This adds a statistical layer to your correlation-based decision.

Plotting out the relationship your variable has with the outcome also allows you to have a visual of the correlation. Excel allows you to add and test the fit (linear, quadratic, etc.). Excel also allows you to quickly and easily filter or build separate tabs for certain years and populations to identify trends and multiple Models that are required to accurately predict the outcome.

Incremen	Ave		Pearson		Increment	Ave		Pearson		Increments	Ave		Pearson
10	35.8	R	0.42		0.1	0.5	R	-0.64		1	2.8	R	0.33
		Pairs	33				Pairs	33				Pairs	33
		T Test	2.59				T Test	4.69				T Test	1.97
		P Value	0.0145				P Value	5.2E-05				P Value	0.0583
		Sig.	Yes				Sig.	Yes				Sig.	No
		Correla	Moderate				Correlat	Strong				Correla	Moderate

Data 1 IV100Pt					Data 2					Data 3 IVPt				
Value	Count	Percent	% Obser	% Predic	Value	Count	Percent	% Obser	% Predic	Value	Count	Percent	% Obser	% Predic
Total	33	100%	36%	100%	Total	33	100%	36%	100%	Total	33	100%	36%	100%
Blank	0	0%	-	-	Blank	0	0%	-	-	Blank	0	0%	-	-
0	2	6%	0%	100%	0%	1	3%	100%	100%	1	8	24%	13%	-
1	1	3%	0%	100%	10%	4	12%	75%	100%	2	6	18%	33%	100%
10	4	12%	0%	100%	20%	4	12%	75%	100%	3	7	21%	43%	100%
20	6	18%	33%	100%	30%	5	15%	60%	100%	4	8	24%	38%	100%
30	6	18%	33%	100%	40%	3	9%	33%	100%	5	4	12%	75%	100%
40	3	9%	33%	100%	50%	4	12%	25%	100%	6	0	0%	-	-
50	2	6%	50%	100%	60%	3	9%	0%	100%		0	0%	-	-
60	4	12%	75%	100%	70%	3	9%	0%	100%		0	0%	-	-
70	4	12%	75%	100%	80%	3	9%	0%	100%		0	0%	-	-
80	1	3%	0%	100%	90%	3	9%	0%	100%		0	0%	-	-
90	0	0%	-	-	100%	0	0%	-	-		0	0%	-	-
100	0	0%	-	-	110%	0	0%	-	-		0	0%	-	-

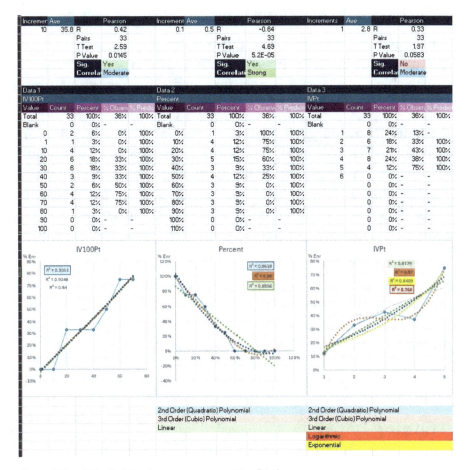

Consider Variable Importance Techniques:

- **Recursive Feature Elimination (RFE)**: This helps determine which variables contribute most to model performance.

- **Lasso Regression**: Lasso can help with variable selection by penalizing the regression model for including too many variables and shrinking some coefficients to zero.

Stepwise Regression: Use forward selection, backward elimination, or stepwise selection to iteratively build your model by adding or removing variables based on their statistical significance or improvement in model fit (e.g., AIC/BIC criteria).

Multivariate Impact: While correlation with the outcome is useful, always consider how variables perform when combined. A variable with weak correlation on its own might become highly valuable when other variables are included in the model.

Domain Knowledge: Sometimes, variables that don't seem strongly correlated with the outcome might be conceptually important based on domain knowledge (e.g., demographic factors that influence admissions behavior), and could be considered despite weak correlation in the existing training data.

Feature Engineering: Some variables may not themselves be strong predictors of the outcome, but when viewed in the context or relationship of another variable, they become a crucial data point. Perhaps the date the student applied does not add to your model, but what if they applied right after visiting campus or signed up for a visit the day they received the Admit/ Aid Award/Transfer Evaluation?

Training Data

As you begin exploring your data, there are some considerations that you should keep in mind.

Historical Data: 3-5 years of data is often a sweet spot for many Predictive Models in admissions. This provides enough history to capture trends and variation while remaining recent enough to reflect current behaviors. However, always consider factors like stability of patterns, external changes, and data volume specific to your institution.

"Stability" is a stretch at the time of writing this book. Between the differences in offerings, timing, and student situations around the COVID 19 Pandemic, FAFSA "Simplification", Demographics and Search Cliffs, questions of the value and

Values of higher education, and alternatives to the traditional college experience, any given year might have trouble generalizing and predicting future years.

1. Consistency of Patterns

- **Stability Over Time**: If the application and enrollment patterns at your institution have remained stable (e.g., admissions policies, marketing strategies, or external factors like the economy haven't drastically changed), using more years of data (~5 years) can be beneficial. This provides a more comprehensive understanding of typical behaviors and reduces the influence of outlier years.

- **Changing Behavior**: If there have been significant changes in recruitment strategies, admissions policies, external factors (e.g., pandemic), or shifts in the student population, you may want to focus on more recent data (~2 years). Older data could introduce bias because it might not reflect current behaviors or trends.

2. Volume of Data

- **Low Volume of Applicants**: If you have fewer applicants and enrollees each year, using more years of data (up to 5-7 years) may be necessary to ensure that your models are trained on a sufficient number of data points. Binary logistic regression models need enough events to make stable predictions.

- **High Volume of Applicants**: If you have a large number of applications or enrollments per year, you can more easily afford to use fewer years of data (e.g., 2-3 years) since each year provides more robust data for training. A common rule of thumb is 10 events per predictor, but some research I have seen recommends up to 50 events. In the case of enrollment Modeling, if you have a 20% yield rate, you would want 10 enrolling students (the least common event) per predictor - 500 admits, 20% (100) enrolling with 10 predictors, so 10 enrolling students per predictor.

3. Changing External Conditions

- **External Trends**: Consider external factors such as economic shifts, demographic changes, or political policies that may impact application and enrollment decisions. If recent trends are particularly relevant (e.g., post-pandemic admissions behavior), you may want to focus on the last 2-3 years of data to reflect current realities.

- **Institutional Changes**: If your institution has made major changes (e.g., changed admissions requirements, introduced new programs, or revised financial aid policies), it's important to use data from after those changes took effect. Including data from before these changes could skew your model.

4. Data Recency and Predictive Power

- **Recency of Data**: More recent data tends to have greater predictive power when forecasting short-term outcomes like likelihood to apply or enroll. Applicant behavior and enrollment decisions can be influenced by shifting social, political, or economic conditions, so older data may not be as predictive for future admissions cycles.

- **Trade-off**: There's a balance between including enough historical data to capture reliable patterns and ensuring the data is recent enough to reflect current behavior. Typically, 3-5 years is a good balance, depending on the stability of your institution's admissions trends.

5. Model Complexity and Overfitting

- **Overfitting Risk**: Using too many years of data can lead to overfitting, where the model learns idiosyncratic details that apply only to past data but not to future applicants. This is especially true if there have been significant changes over time.

- **Underfitting Risk**: On the other hand, using too few years may lead to underfitting, where the model does not capture important longer-term trends and variabilities in the data.

6. Cross-Validation and Backtesting

- **Cross-Validation**: You can use cross-validation (e.g., k-fold) to test how your models perform using different subsets of your data, ensuring the model generalizes well across different years.

- **Backtesting**: Simulate predictions by using older years of data to predict subsequent years. For example, train on data from 2018-2020 and predict behavior in 2021. This helps assess whether including more years of data improves predictive accuracy.

7. Practical Considerations

1. **Availability of Data**: Use as many years of data as are available and relevant. If historical data is incomplete, has changed formats, or lacks critical variables, it might not be worth including.

2. **Data Granularity**: If you have very detailed data on applicant behavior (e.g., Engagement Scores, web interactions, etc.), fewer years might still provide enough richness for the model to learn from.

Missing Data

Depending on the variables in the model, there may also be some missing data - GPA, changes in behavior opportunities (virtual/in person events during the pandemic, new forms, etc.), and other issues. Binary logistic regression will exclude those records with missing data from the training data. And applying the model to current records missing data (multiplying by 0 essentially) could drastically change student probabilities when a missing data strategy could give you much more accurate predictions.

There are a few plans. Maybe not fun or fast, but there are plans. Investigation as to why the data is missing should always be performed. If a process is broken, incomplete, or missing an element that will bring in the data, that should be updated. But if data is truly missing, then let's look at some of those plans -

1. **Exclusion:** Exclude records with missing data from your analysis/future records being predicted on. This is fast and tempting, but as with many fast and tempting options, probably won't serve the institution best. Students with missing data are likely an important element of your population and training data, so excluding them will harm your model and its generalizability. And excluding/mispredicting live records again will harm any predictions you're trying to make, possibly to the point where the model may do

more harm than good.

2. **Replaced Valued**: Replacing null values for variables like missing GPA with a static value or population average would preserve these records for use in the training data and allow the model automation to work on the record. Coalescing (creating a series of variables that will be used if the previous is missing/null) this data in a Slate export is still within our Quickster's fast and easy super powers to do in the Automation Queries or in a Rule/separate Query writing to a Field if the computational power can't be spared in the Automation Query

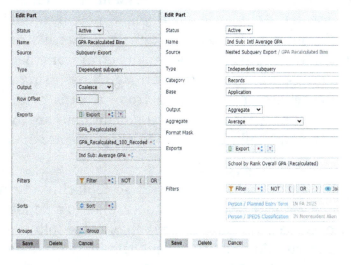

3.   **Predictive Values:** Creating additional regressions to predict the null values based on other data and engagement behaviors. These imputational regressions can again be run in the Slate queries or in separate Rules/Queries to write to a field specifically designed to hold imputed variables. You don't want to report predicted GPA just because you put it in the standard field for use in Predictive Modeling.

While regression-based imputation is the most time-consuming

option, that is a much better way to balance your model and account for the inconsistencies in your data, especially if you are including Pandemic-era data in your model where you're likely to have a broad range of expected values that are very nuanced.

Think predicting in-person attendance for students whose recruitment cycle happened when there were no (or limited) in-person events. If you include event attendance in your model, these people will be coded as 0 (or null depending on your query). In your training data, that will pull your effect size for attendance towards 0.

Some of these people would have visited your campus if they had the chance. So if you use a regression based on other Slate data to predict attendance, then you'll more accurately build your main outcome model. Additional touches like Stochastic Regression Imputation (adding random error from the residuals of the model) and Predictive Mean Matching (using observed values to replace missing data from records with similar predicted means) may increase data quality but are more time consuming and would be harder to program into Slate to run automatically.

The lower entry plans would include replacing the missing datapoints with an average of the remaining population or some otherwise determined static value. These solutions would not require running additional models in SPSS. In fact, they can be calculated in Slate, even tailoring the averages live with independent subqueries. But this plan is far hollower than the imputational regressions, which will likely give you more accurate predictions. There are other methods, but these are a good starting point with a broad level of intensity.

Conclusion

Effective Predictive Modeling requires a nuanced approach to data selection and variable importance, grounded in both statistical methods and domain knowledge. By being mindful of overfitting and avoiding the temptation to go fishing for correlations, you can enhance the Model's predictive power. Addressing issues like missing data thoughtfully ensures broader applicability. These strategies will help you build robust Models that accurately reflect your institution's unique context and adapt to the evolving landscape of higher education.

CHAPTER 8: TRAINING DATA
PART 2: CONSIDERATIONS

There are several broader decisions that you will have to continue making with your training data and records. These will influence how you select, code, and clean your data. This includes handling unique populations and bias. These will be essential in not creating accurate but also responsible models that will contribute to student and institutional success.

Changes In Behaviors

The COVID 19 pandemic offers a clear example for our first topic. Many institutions that offer gap years saw a dramatic increase in them (same for leaves of absence). A use case for your Modeling may be enrollment at Census to plan and project for headcount and Net Tuition Revenue. In which case, a gap year student is coded as non-enrolling despite the fact they may look more like an enrolling student. This noise is tempered by a small number of students in this group.

During the pandemic though, when gap years increased tenfold (or whatever your scenario was), this noise can poison your model. This substantive shift in outcome behaviors posed a serious issue in the training data, so for that year, these gap year students could be coded as enrolling students to improve the model accuracy.

There is an easy argument that a student taking a gap year looks more like an enrolling student than others who do not yield. But since this model was for predicting headcounts and Net Tuition Revenue as of census, it was more important to focus on predicting that census date, even if the model was slightly noisier for it. These are the kind of "game day decisions" that you will need to decide when crafting your model(s). Trends may emerge over the course of your training data, so aggregating to the mean may miss nuances of future students for the sake of Modeling.

Populations

Predictive Modeling in higher education, particularly for admission and enrollment outcomes, relies on analyzing historical data to predict future behaviors. However, not all datapoints or populations provide useful signals to the model, and in some cases, including certain populations can distort the results, reducing the overall predictive accuracy. It is critical to carefully consider which populations should be excluded from the training data. Excellent examples would be stealth applicants and waitlist admits.

Stealth Applicants: Excluding Populations Without Behavioral Data

Stealth applicants are those who submit applications without displaying any prior behaviors that can be tracked by the CRM system. These students aren't engaging with recruitment emails, attending events, or visiting the campus prior to applying, which means they leave no trace in the engagement data that is needed to build a predictive model.

Including these students in a model trained to predict broader application behavior can introduce unnecessary noise. The model cannot generalize to this population because there are no predictors that help explain their decision to apply. In essence, they are anomalies in the data that are unpredictable by the very nature of their behavior, or lack thereof. So trying to train or apply the model on these records would likely reduce the accuracy of the model, leading to weaker predictions for engaged prospects, which form a core population of interest for most institutions.

Waitlist Admits: A Special Case in Enrollment Modeling

Another population that may be excluded from Predictive Models focused on enrollment outcomes are waitlist admits. This exclusion becomes particularly important when the model is built on pre-decision data, where the goal is to predict whether an admitted student will enroll based on their behaviors and characteristics prior to receiving an offer of admission.

Waitlist admits represent a distinct scenario because their enrollment decisions are often influenced by a different set of factors compared to regular admits. For instance, a student admitted from the waitlist might have already mentally committed to another institution or may be more inclined to accept the offer due to its late timing. Their decision-making process is therefore distinct from students who receive a traditional offer of admission.

In Models built on pre-decision data, including waitlist admits could introduce noise because their behavior, prior to receiving an offer, may not be comparable to other admits in relation to their decision to enroll. Since the model is trying to learn patterns in behavior that predict whether a student will enroll, having a subset of the population with a different set of decision-making criteria can skew the model's predictions. This can lead to a decrease in model accuracy and an inability to generalize well to the broader admit population.

The Role Of Outliers

Outliers - students that deviate significantly from the average behavior - pose another challenge when training predictive models. While it might seem tempting to remove outliers to create a cleaner dataset, it's important to consider their story and whether that's where the story should end. Outliers can represent rare but important cases that could be informative if handled correctly.

When deciding whether to remove outliers, ask: What is their data story? Are they outliers because they represent a specific, unmodeled phenomenon, or are they simply random noise? For example, if a particular applicant or group of applicants has a set of behaviors that are vastly different from the typical population, it could indicate that something significant is happening - such as a new trend in how certain students engage with the admissions process. In this case, rather than removing them, it might be more appropriate to investigate these behaviors and account for them in the model, either by segmenting this group into an additional model or incorporating additional/engineered variables.

On the other hand, outliers can sometimes be the result of data errors, missing information, or rare events that do not generalize to the broader population. In these cases, removing them can help the model avoid overfitting to peculiarities in the historical data, thus improving its ability to generalize to new, unseen cases.

Preventing Overfitting: Balancing Data

One of the central goals when training predictive models is to avoid overfitting—where the model learns patterns that are specific to the training data but do not generalize to new data. Removing populations like stealth applicants, waitlist admits, and extreme outliers can help prevent overfitting by ensuring that the model is not overly influenced by patterns that do not apply to the majority of the future students. But overfitting can also happen when over-engineering a model to describe every bit of variance you can.

However, it is also important not to be too aggressive in removing datapoints. Sometimes, outliers or unique populations can provide valuable insight into behaviors that may become more common in the future. For example, if stealth applications are becoming a growing trend, it might be worth developing a separate model specifically for this population or creating a hybrid model that accounts for both engaged and stealth applicants in a balanced way.

Removing certain populations and data from Predictive Modeling is not only about cleaning the dataset but ensuring that the model can generalize well to future populations and solve the question or problem your institution has. Stealth applicants and waitlist admits represent specific groups that are difficult to model based on typical engagement and pre-decision data, respectively, and including them can introduce noise that distorts predictions. Outliers, while often seen as troublesome, have their own data story and may either need to be excluded or handled in a way that prevents overfitting while still accounting for important, albeit rare, behaviors. The key is to strike a balance between refining the data and ensuring the model is robust, flexible, and capable of making accurate predictions for the institution's primary populations.

Dangers Of Bias And Adverse Impact

Bias in predictive models can result in adverse impact, where certain groups are disproportionately harmed by model decisions. In the context of admissions, this may mean that applicants from underrepresented groups are less likely to be admitted, not because they are less qualified, but because the model is trained on biased data.

For example, models that favor high test scores or extracurricular involvement may disadvantage students from low-income backgrounds, who might not have had access to test preparation services or extracurricular activities but will be successful at your institutions.

Similarly, models trained on historical data where certain demographics were underrepresented may continue to predict lower chances of success for students from these backgrounds, thus reinforcing patterns of exclusion.

Negative outcomes of current students for only a handful in a population may skew predictions on student success and retention, especially when they come from a small population. These students may have faced a cultural issue, problems with a particular student, staff, or faculty member, or some other barrier that is not on due to the student. And if this success Model is used to direct admission decisions, prospective students that have similar predictors may not receive proper consideration.

Moreover, bias in admissions models can have long-term consequences, perpetuating inequality not just within the institution but also in society. Students who are denied access to education due to biased models may miss out on opportunities that could have altered their socioeconomic trajectory, thus deepening societal divisions.

A thorough examination and understanding of the training data is needed with special awareness to smaller groups that are especially susceptible to issues in the Predictive Modeling process.

Scores and Models should be regularly audited for bias, both during development and after implementation. Bias audits involve assessing the model's predictions to identify any disproportionate impact on specific groups. If adverse impact is detected, you should adjust your models accordingly, either by retraining the model or by applying post-processing techniques to ensure fair outcomes.

Mitigating Bias in Predictive Models

Addressing bias and adverse impact in predictive models starts with a commitment to ethical data practices. There are several strategies that you can employ to reduce bias in your models:

Diverse and Representative Data Collection: You should strive to collect data from a wide range of student populations, ensuring that your models are trained on data that reflects the diversity of the applicant pool. This may involve supplementing historical data with more recent or targeted data collection efforts to ensure that all groups are adequately represented.

Feature Selection and Engineering: Careful attention should be paid to the selection of features used in the model. In some cases, these features may need to be excluded or adjusted to prevent the Model from relying on biased patterns. Feature engineering can also be used to create variables that emphasize merit and potential rather than circumstances beyond a student's control.

Fairness-Aware Algorithms: Using fairness-aware algorithms, which are designed to minimize bias in predictions, can be an effective approach. These algorithms can help ensure that certain groups are not systematically disadvantaged by the model's predictions. Techniques like reweighting or re-sampling the training data to ensure balanced representation across different groups can also be employed.

Regular Bias Audits: Predictive Models should be regularly audited for bias, both during development and after implementation. Bias audits involve assessing the model's predictions to identify any disproportionate impact on specific groups. If adverse impact is detected, you should adjust your models accordingly, either by retraining the model or by applying post-processing techniques to ensure fair outcomes.

Explainability and Transparency: You should ensure that the decision-making processes of your predictive models are transparent. By making models explainable, decision-makers can better understand how and why the model makes certain predictions, which can help identify sources of bias. Additionally, transparency fosters trust in the system, as stakeholders can see that steps are being taken to ensure fairness.

Involving Diverse Stakeholders: Finally, involving a diverse group of stakeholders in the model development process can help identify potential biases that may not be immediately apparent. By bringing together individuals from different backgrounds and perspectives, you can better ensure that your models account for a wide range of experiences and do not inadvertently disadvantage any particular group.

Conclusion

Effective Predictive Modeling requires a balanced approach that combines statistical rigor with ethical responsibility. By carefully selecting data, thoughtfully managing unique populations, and addressing outliers, you enhance Model accuracy and relevance.

Bias and adverse impact in predictive models for higher education admissions represent serious risks, but they can be mitigated with careful attention to data collection, feature selection, Model choice, and ongoing evaluation. By actively working to minimize bias, you can use predictive models as a tool to promote equity rather than perpetuate inequality, creating more inclusive and fair admissions processes.

CHAPTER 9: IMPLEMENTING AND AUTOMATING THE MODEL

Now that you have a better grasp on the data and considerations around Predictive Modeling, you have a few forks in the road ahead of you. With over a dozen statistical models and machine learning algorithms, you will need to find one that fits the outcomes you need, maps well to your data and staffing expertise, and fits within your technical limitations. From there, you will need systems to not only build but run your Model. While your Model may inform these decisions, if your systems are a limitation, then finding the right model that can be run, implemented, and used may be a decision for the end of this road.

For the purposes of this book, we will be using SPSS to build a Binary Logistic Regression Model. The model will then be replicated in Slate to run and apply to your records automatically in a similar process to Engagement Scoring in Act I. This process includes transforming your model results into a 0-100% likelihood Score.

Choosing Between Spss And R (Or Other Systems)

One of the first major decisions when building a Predictive Model is selecting the right system for Modeling and execution. Building the model requires statistics software like SPSS, Stata, SAS, or R. Many institutions have licenses for SPSS, and staff are more likely to have been trained on SPSS. R is a great, open source, and free alternative that is far more robust in its total possible functionality, especially with machine learning algorithms. The best analogy for Slate users would be that:

- SPSS is the Standard Template Library. Much easier to stand up and run with. Preset user interface and functionality.

- R is writing your query in SQL (not to be confused with the fact that the programming language for R is extremely similar to Python). The sky is the limit... if you already know how to fly.

- RStudio is a combination of Configurable Joins and Suitcases. Better interface than a blank screen. Open-source packages help with the lift. Learning curve is still steep compared to SPSS.

R is a powerful, open-source language widely used for statistical computing and machine learning. Commonly photographed in the hands of data scientists because it offers a vast number of packages that support sophisticated algorithms and statistical models. However, R comes with a steeper learning curve, particularly for users who may not have a programming background. R's syntax-heavy interface, while flexible and scalable, can be intimidating.

Alternatively, SPSS is a robust, user-friendly statistical analysis tool that many professionals in higher education are already familiar with. One of the primary advantages of SPSS is its intuitive graphical user interface (GUI), which allows users to perform complex analyses without needing to code. In SPSS, you can select your data, run models, and produce results through a series of clicks. Paste-ing these operations or learning the syntax behind the operations does offset some of the advantages of R, but only partially at that.

For the purposes of this book, we will focus on using SPSS to build our Predictive Models, given that many participants already have experience with this software. However, for those interested in learning R, keep in mind that it's an excellent tool for expanding your skills in machine learning and advanced statistical Modeling.

SPSS: Interacting with the Software

SPSS is designed to be as user-friendly as possible, with a few key window types that you'll interact with:

Data View: This is similar to a spreadsheet where you input and manage your dataset. Before you can begin building a model, you need to ensure your data is structured properly.

Variable View: This is where you define the characteristics of each variable in your dataset. You can label variables, define variable types, and set value labels.

Output View: This is where SPSS shows the results of your analysis. Whenever you run a model, SPSS will generate tables, charts, and statistics here.

Syntax View: This is the hidden gem of SPSS. While the GUI is a fantastic tool for those who prefer a click-based interface, syntax allows users to write or paste code that centralizes repetitive, slow tasks and reduces errors.

Integrating Predictive Models With Slate

Predictive Models are only as impactful as their ability to be deployed. After you've built your model in SPSS and generated the unstandardized regression coefficients, you'll want to program the math into Slate to automate predictions for current and future students. Slate offers seamless capabilities for importing and exporting data as well as running models internally, making it an ideal platform for higher education Predictive Modeling.

If you are using a separate system or CRM but still want to run the model in-system, ensure it can export/import data and perform calculations in a formula like SQL.

For Slate, this involves using Configurable Joins to aggregate behaviors and data for Predictive Modeling and to export the training data.

Much of the Slate-side of this build uses the same process of automated Engagement Scoring by exporting the data in Slate Queries and re-importing them automatically every weekend with a Source Format.

Because Slate has to replicate not only the behavior counts but also the math of the Binary Logistic Regression, this will take a couple more rounds of Queries/Source Formats. Not to worry, This just involves a little copy and pasting from your SPSS results into Slate formulas.

After running the binary logistic regression in SPSS. You

will need the unstandardized regression coefficients. These represent the change in the log-odds of the outcome for a one-unit increase in the predictor variable, holding other variables constant. These coefficients show how each predictor influences the likelihood of the binary event occurring without being scaled. You will get a table like the one pictured.

		B	S.E.	Wald	df	Sig.	Exp(B)	95% C.I.for EXP(B) Lower	Upper
								95% C.I.for EXP(B)	
Step 1[a]	IV100Pt	4.96779	640.271	.000	1	.994	143.708	.000	.
	IV5Pt	-7.79237	2381.102	.000	1	.997	.000	.000	.
	IV2Pt(1)	-32.40123	8896.086	.000	1	.997	.000	.000	.
	IV1Pt(1)	-24.24786	7946.572	.000	1	.998	.000	.000	.
	Constant	-184.53242	25496.883	.000	1	.994	.000		

Variables in the Equation

a. Variable(s) entered on step 1: IV100Pt, IV5Pt, IV2Pt, IV1Pt.

With standalone Slate fields (meticulously named as described in the Scoring Shapter) created for each of your behavior, your first query calculates the number of each behavior or the appropriate datapoints. Examples of this can be seen in the Feature Engineering Chapter.

The second query calculates the logit. This is the natural logarithm of the odds ratio of an event occurring versus not occurring. It transforms probabilities (bounded between 0 and 1) into a continuous range, allowing a linear relationship between predictor variables and the log-odds of the binary outcome. Don't worry, this is not what your staff will be using.

This is where you need your SPSS values. In a Slate Formula Export, add your constant value, essentially the default value of the student before any behaviors are added. Then you will sum the parenthetical value of the students' datapoints multiplied by the unstandardized regression weight - the capital B in the SPSS table. Do this for each of the behaviors in your model.

If you are running multiple models - one set of variables and weights for domestic students, another set for students on financial aid, etc., create Exports in your Query for each of these models to run them all at the same time.

The third Query in the sequence creates your 0-100% probability. You have to take Euler's Number (2.718281828) and exponentiate it to your Logit. Divide that by 1 + the same thing.

Again, do this in the same Query for each of your enrollment models to cut down on the number of Queries running.

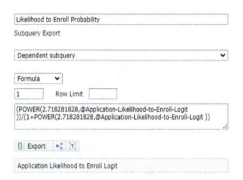

If there are multiple models, then one additional Query is needed to aggregate the models to create a central probability of each student to enroll. Coalesce these model aggregates

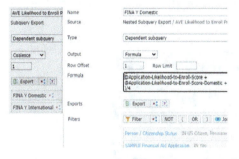

Each aggregate averages the relevant models. Adding Filters allows the single Coalesce Export to write the appropriate probability for each student regardless of which populations they fall into.

In that short sequence of Queries, you went from raw behaviors to a 0-100% likelihood written directly to each student's Slate fields. Because the actual math is relatively simple, the Models can also be created in a Report to get live results. Which means you can craft your class live in Slate and project how nudges and anticipated action would affect your results as the individual, population, and class-levels.

Automating Model Updates

While presenting on this process at places like Slate Summit and AACRAO SEM, and the Empowering Admission Workshop series, it always felt like this element was overshadowed. Building the model is great, applying it to your records is also great, but then Slate automatically refreshes how likely your prospect will perform your outcome behavior all year long. They visited campus this week? They are 4 percent more likely to matriculate. The next week they sent you another email? 1.2 percent more likely to enroll. And if it's not a priority or possibility to update your model each year, then Slate will continue to refresh its predictions on all of your records forever.

For a one-time lift.

Before I start sounding like a snake oil salesman, Models do need to be updated. Binary Logistic Regression requires accurate records and behaviors, and the changing landscape of higher education and institution practice and policy can make older records less valuable in Modeling future behaviors. These older records engage differently with the institution (and may not have engaged at all in new practices coded into the model). There may be other factors that are not in Slate that will reduce the value in the model.

Not only will these older records affect the accuracy of your Predictive Modeling, but also the consistency of your student populations. When building this predictive model at a highly selective, small, liberal arts college, the school's popularity was actually a hindrance to the Modeling. Students showing very low demonstrated interest as captured in Slate enrolled are remarkably high levels. Even stealth applicants whose only interaction with the institution was applying and submitting required materials. Even moderators struggled to ferret out an effective way to identify this group of low-engagement/high-enrollment students.

While those are two things more out of the Model builder's control. Selecting the "right" behaviors and other datapoints being added are critically important. As is the proper coding of the behaviors. The model will functionally work regardless of the quality or number of variables. If there is only one variable - a domestic/international flag, and domestic students historically enroll 45% of the time and international students historically enroll 40% of the time, then Slate will look at if they are domestic or not and apply those %s to them. Could be valuable, but there's so much more context you could add (and you also don't need Binary Logistic Modeling for this). On the other hand, adding 30 variables, some being significant predictors and some not, may not be optimal at predicting future student behavior.

There is significant nuance to the process. If your Slate team does not have the required knowledge, an IR Office or faculty may be able to assist with this side of the process.

Note: Data is a great element to add to your business process, but avoiding technical debt in the process by the way of automation can drive better, next generation outcomes.

To ensure that predictions remain updated to recent behaviors, you can schedule each of the above Queries to run to your SFTP server. Use Slate's Schedule Export feature in Queries to automate execution at regular intervals. This ensures that probabilities are updated, reflecting the latest student interactions. Some recommendations:

Note that the path needs "../incoming/" to place the query results in the "Incoming" folder which is where the Source Format will need them to be to pick the file up and import it.

Set up an email to receive notification for at least Failures and late deliveries.

Schedule the more intensive queries for slower days/times if possible. If there are multiple queries that need to run, staggering the windows will help error-proof your sequence rather than trying to ingest them in the appropriate order in the same window.

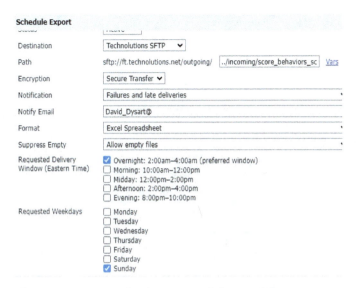

You can then automate the import of data with a Source Format. There are a few notes:

On the General Tab - Set Status to Active, give it a descriptive Name, Remap As Of to capture the earliest file and set Remap Active to Active, Set to Unsafe so current Applicants can have fields updated (even if you think you set your new fields to Unsafe), set Update Only, and set Notifications to at least email relevant staff on Failures. Adjust other settings as needed.

General	Format Definition	Import Automation

Status	Active ▾
Name	Engagement Score - Behaviors
Format	xlsx
Type	One-Time / Differential
	Existing sources in this format will be retair
Remap As Of Date	2024-05-29
Remap Active	Active ▾
	When this flag is active, data for existing fi Awaiting Import will be imported using the confirm your remap settings prior to activa
Scope	Person/Dataset Record ▾
Dataset	Person/Application Records ▾
Unsafe	Unsafe
Hide	Create source interactions ▾
Disable Update Queue	Allow records to enter update queue upor
Update Only	Update only ▾
Notification	Failures only ▾
Notification Email	David_Dysart@

Under the Format Definition Tab, this code in the XML box tells Slate that the first row in your file is the Header with Column Names

<layout type="convert" h="1" />

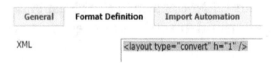

General	Format Definition	Import Automation
XML		<layout type="convert" h="1" />

The last important piece to update is in the Import Automation Tab. You must add the name specified in the Query's Scheduled Export. This tells Slate what file to pick up and ingest. This example uses an asterisk wildcard to look for the file name and any additional text where the "*" is at. This is important if you are adding a timestamp.

If you have multiple Scheduled Exports that may be picked up, you will need to revise your naming convention. "model_enroll*.xlsx" would pick up all three of these files:

model_enroll_behaviors.xlsx

model_enroll_logit.xlsx

model_enroll_probability.xlsx

General	Format Definition	Import Automation

Import Path/Mask	score_behaviors_score*.xlsx

By automating model calculations, admissions teams can focus on interpreting the data and making informed decisions, rather than manually updating Scores to upkeep external systems and integrations.

Conclusion

The process of creating a binary logistic regression Model in SPSS as well as transforming it in Slate is probably the lowest hanging branch to get into Predictive Modeling for higher education. Because of its interpretability and lower computation cost, it's also extremely flexible and adaptable for a whole suite of initiatives and strategies we will discuss in Act III.

While advanced algorithms offer significant potential, starting with accessible tools ensures immediate impact and scalability. As the landscape evolves, institutions equipped with these foundational models will be well-positioned to adopt more sophisticated approaches when ready and needed.

CHAPTER 10: TIME-SPECIFIC ANCHORS AND MODELS

In the context of higher education enrollment, time-anchored data and timestamping behaviors is essential for creating accurate and reliable predictions. By focusing on the precise timing of student interactions relative to outcomes like application submission or enrollment, institutions can avoid weaker predictors and underperforming models. We'll explore strategies for handling timestamped behaviors and how both multiple models and multiple versions of a model can improve outcomes for your students and institution.

Depending on the use of your model, you may need to timestamp your data and behaviors to accurately train your model. If you are Modeling on how likely a prospective student is to apply, you don't want to train a model based on behaviors like sending emails AFTER they have already applied. Similarly, if you are trying to predict the enrollment likelihood of admitted students at time of admission, then you don't want to include that Admitted Student Day (or other events) in your training data.

Unsurprisingly, matriculating students tend to eventually engage in more behaviors than just applicants. Applicants will also inherently have higher behavior counts than prospective students as they have more reason, time, opportunities, and programming to do so.

But the flexibility of Configurable Joins Queries can accommodate this. Compare timestamps of the behaviors relative to the outcome in question. For applicant Modeling, pull variables at time of application (or application deadline for non-applicants). Depending on your use, the app deadline for both groups may be more appropriate. This screenshot example shows the Subquery Export's Filter.

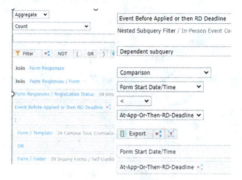

Coalescing the date filter (if Application date is blank, move to the next criteria such as the application deadline) pulls these apps and non-apps in the same query run with the appropriate behavior counts, so it is not much more complicated* to use both application timestamp and application deadline than applying the application deadline for all records.

Note: The Joins Juggler understands that when David says "not much more complicated" that it is relative. Running additional nested exports that include Coalesces and written formulas can be substantially different that other Configurable Joins being used. David can just be as short-sighted as his glasses prescription.

Similarly, for enrollment Modeling that I typically reference in this book, Slate uses behaviors as of decision release by the institution. While matriculation predictions could be more accurate if they used behaviors at time of committing, deadline to commit, or even census, this use case is particularly interested in using the probability to enroll at time of decision committee to inform census headcount and net tuition revenue projections. That way, it was tailored to admitting the correct number of applicants to achieve the needed incoming class.

The above pictures are a good guide to start building the query. It is a bit blunt and may miss records with wandering entry terms (changing their planned entry term, multiple applications, etc.), so if that is a substantial population for the institution, a more refined process of pulling historical data per cycle to build the model may be needed.

You will need to be thoughtful of what the main use cases are for these models and what decisions will... yield the most impactful data. Multiple versions of the models can be created with an incremental additional lift (less than the 9-model solution above). The variables for an enrollment model at time of admission committee and an enrollment model at time of census could have heavy overlap.

In Elaboratione (Latin for "In Elaboration" where I will expand and offer some additional guidance instead of finding a better place for the topic to live in the book.)

On the topic of Multiple Models and Multiple Versions

It may be helpful to distinguish multiple models and multiple versions. I advocate for multiple models regardless. This could be averaging across several models relevant to a student. If they are an International STEM Student on Financial Aid who submitted a Stealth Application (applied without engaging with the institution), each of these factors may have a separate Model with their own predictors and weights -

- STEM Model: 80% likely to enroll.

- International Model: 70% likely to enroll.

- Financial Aid Model: 65% likely to enroll.

- Stealth Applicant Model: 85% likely to enroll.

- Aggregated Predicted: 75% likely to enroll.

This is analogous to DIY-ing your own (simplified) Random Forest Model. Understanding how their different aspects contribute to their final outcome of enrolling allows you to better predict the individual's action (and how the broader population will behave). Adding additional segments like a "STEM and on Financial Aid" may struggle unless you have a large dataset to work with. And adding a poor Model may contaminate your predictions.

You may find that the additional predictive power is not worth the time to build and maintain multiple Models. You may also be able to account for some differences with standalone predictors and interaction/moderator effects. Ultimately, when it's your flying monkeys, it's also your circus (or in this case, twisted, non-Euclidean castle set high atop the cliffs).

It may also serve your institution to have multiple VERSIONS of your models. Your model predicting enrollment at time of decision release may be an important element of your practices, but a month after decisions, that model does not distinguish how a student's behaviors since decisions will influence the likelihood of enrolling.

Creating an additional Model(s) that includes additional/different factors may help guide yield efforts and Waitlist offers, so depending on resources, needs, and goals, it may be important for your institution to create these additional Models. It could be prudent to pilot the first Model(s) and then each cycle, add Models as needed to address the gaps at your institution. This could also be a good opportunity to experiment with different types of Models/Algorithms to find the best versions for your institution or specific use cases.

This second version of enrollment Modeling would require a second query with the proper timestamp comparison and different model values that get plugged into Slate queries (remember when I said naming your fields would be VERY important). Feature-engineering additional behaviors around institutional actions like decision/transfer evaluation, aid awards would likely pose the largest tasks as nothing particularly similar would have been created for a At Decision Model.

Terminus: In Elaboratione (Latin for "End: In Elaboration")

Conclusion

Effective Predictive Modeling in higher education requires a precise understanding of time-anchored data and student behaviors, allowing institutions to tailor models accurately to various outcomes. By creating models and versions that adapt to unique timestamps and student actions, enrollment managers can make data-informed decisions, enhancing outreach, admissions strategies, and yield management. Thoughtful model design and multiple iterations enable institutions to support students more effectively while meeting enrollment goals with greater precision.

CHAPTER 11: FEATURE ENGINEERING

The data available to you for Predictive Modeling grows exponentially the longer you are on Slate and the more integrated it is with your student experience. Feature engineering plays a critical role in enhancing the performance of Predictive Models though. Utilizing Configurable Joins and building robust models that reflect the realities of student engagement over time and around important moments that matter, your model and actions can become exponentially more impactful.

I will use the term "feature engineering" relatively broadly in the book. In general, it involves transforming raw data into meaningful predictors that improve model performance. This process includes creating, modifying, or selecting variables that capture important patterns, relationships, or trends in the data, ultimately helping the model better predict outcomes by enhancing its ability to recognize key insights.

The Predictive Modeling I'm covering in this book is designed to be replicated and automated in Slate, so I will be limiting our examples to what can be done in Configurable Joins and in Export Formulas (essentially SQL with only a smaller selection of functions). While there are much more extensive transformations that can be done on your data with the final value being imported into Slate, that's another topic for another book. Let's explore a few different ways to manipulate your Slate data. Some of these variables may lend themselves more to Engagement Scoring or other flags to drive institutional action.

Capping Behaviors (Logins)

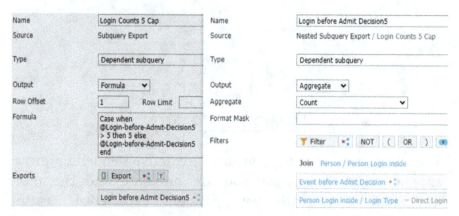

In this Export, you are Aggregating the Count (summing the number of times a behavior occurred). In this case, the number of times a student logged into the portal, though this could be anything from attending events, sending emails, time on the website with Ping, etc.

Since you are counting the number of portal logins, you also need to restrict it to Direct Logins to exclude any staff impersonations. And again, we are looking specifically at the number of times before the Admit decision was released.

After exploring the data, you also determined that the best way to classify the variable was to cap the count at 5. With binary logistic regression, the model establishes a linear relationship between the behaviors and the outcome, so the influence of additional logins increases at the same rate between 0 and the highest observed number (with the increments established in the training data). This could lead to logins taking up all of the oxygen in the model, essentially elevating it to the central behavior beyond its actual predictive ability for most records and vastly skew the probability for your records. If all you need is a raw count of the events, you can removed the Formula layer of this Export and just use the Aggregate.

Note from our resident Field of Statistics Mouse: While in general, it's not usually advisable to limit, dummy code, restrict, etc. data in statistics, a bit of engineering will likely increase the impact of your model. This must be done with great care to prevent overfitting, cherry picking, and dilution of quality. I like to do extensive data exploration to get a feel for variables and their relationship with the outcome to inform transformations.

Flags and Dummy Coding (Event Attendance)

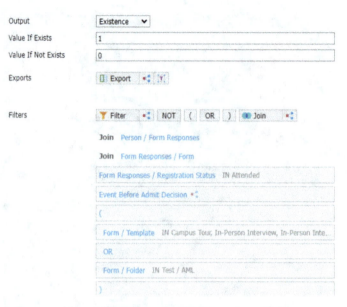

Perhaps the number of events (even restricted) is not as good of an indicator as the existence of an event (or other behavior) at all. The previous formula could be used, but this would be more computationally efficient. It exports a 0 if the student has not attended an event and a 1 if they have. This can be especially helpful when there is a very non-linear relationship between the raw count and the logit of the outcome.

Recent Behaviors (Emails Sent by Student)

This example counts the number of times a behavior like emails sent by the student occurred within the last 30 days. We'll calculate time-relative behaviors differently in another example. The second pop-up has several relevant filters for querying emails sent.

The Method allows you to specify "Email" as opposed to other data on that table like SMS, Letters, Mail Merges, Voice, etc.

The Type also specifies we want External Messages coming into Slate as opposed to Deliver Mailings, Form Communications, and Ad Hoc Messages all sent from Slate.

Lastly, you will want to specify the email address sending the email is the student's email as emails merely attached to the record from parents, counselors, vendors providing material, etc. will also be included without this filter which are not going to be as predictive as actual messages from the student.

Recoding Values (Score Transformations)

Score Recode Reverse A = 2	Name	Score
Subquery Export	Source	Nested Export / SAMPI
Dependent subquery	Aggregate	[▾]
Formula ▾	Export Value	Translation Code ▾
1 Row Limit [ ]	Translation Key	letter_to_number ▾
Case when @Score in (1, 2, 3) then 2 when @Score in (4, 5) then 1	Translation Value	Export Value ▾
	Format Type	Integer
⊞ Export •፧ [T]	Format Mask	[ ]
Score	Null Value	[ ]

This example uses multiple methods and reasons to transform your data. A formula gives you the ability to reverse code your Score. In this case, a 1 in the Score variable is a "better" Score.

Perhaps to make explanation easier, you are using the formula to change the "better" Score to be the "higher" numeric value, so as the student Scores better, their value in this datapoint is higher. It's a more intuitive way to describe the model.

The formula is also recoding the Score to group the values. If the student Scored a "1", "2", or "3", then their new value is a "2". This is likely because those three values have a similar relationship to the outcome while a "4" and "5" share a similar relationship. You would also want to be mindful of size discrepancies between the groups.

Lastly, you are using a Translation Code to transform the raw values of letters into numeric values. In theory, all three of these transformations could be done with a single Translation Code, but that may become too blunt and hyper specific of a use case for an office-available Translation Code.

The current Translation Code is used to convert the letters to numbers which may have several business practices associated with it. If you use a 1 to indicate the best Score as a general practice, you probably don't want to clutter your Translation Code with an Export Value that contradicts how staff will interpret Scores in case they use this Translation Code instead of another that keeps Scoring consistent.

Similarly, if only one model requires this particular translation of "1", "2", and "3" = "2", then you may require several similar Translation Codes and may accidentally update a Report or Query's calculations when updating this Translation Code. So I would recommend controlling your Translations more granularly and clearly.

Translation Codes

Key	letter_to_number
Type	String (Discrete Values)
Default	No default exports have been configured for this key.

Value	Export Value
New Code	
A	1
B	2
C	3
D	4
F	5

Distance Recoding

A student's proximity to campus can impact their probability to apply and enroll in several avenues. Most students attend college in their state. There is some inferential data from vendors that can indicate in/out of state college-going desire and trends. International/domestic is another way to examine probability.

In this example, you are using a formula to examine a couple data elements based on the students distance from the institution. If the school they attend is in the country, then it returns the number of miles the student's school is from the institution. If the school is international or you don't have the address information, then it examines the student's permanent address. If neither are domestic, then the formula just returns a static number of miles.

A Translation Code then categorizes the raw number of miles into three buckets that can be entered into the model as a predictor, interactions effect, or augment a feature. More customization can go into a variable like this depending on how distance-related variables are related to your outcome.

Export Value	Translation Code ▾
Translation Key	campus_distance ▾
Translation Value	Export Value ▾

Translation Codes

Key	campus_distance
Type	Real Number (Inclusive Range of Values)
Default	No default exports have been configured for this key.

Sea

Min Value	Max Value	Export Value
New Code		
0	1000	1
1000.001	3000	2
3000.001	100000	3

Behavioral Changes

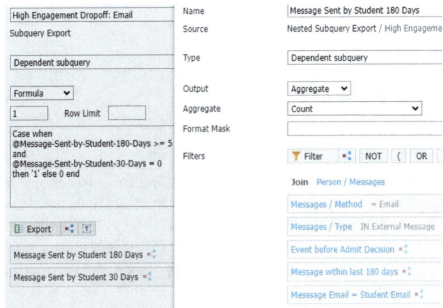

A drastic change in engagement behaviors should set off alarm bells in your office. In this example, the student was highly engaged, sending at least five emails in the last 180 days. But they sent zero emails in the last 30 days. These criteria could also use other anchors like Engagement Score greater than thirty but zero engagements (emails, Ping, events) after Decision Received, Campus tour, Financial Aid Meeting, etc. This could be strongly indicative of a change in enrollment probability. Re-engaging the student could be needed to keep them in the funnel.

Categorizing Behaviors

Institutions send a variety of emails and call-to-actions. A student ignoring an email about how good your weather is or not clicking on an event registration link in it probably isn't the end of the world or their journey with your institution.

But what about those emails and SMSs about missing application materials or onboarding actions? There's a broad spectrum of importance and topics, so being more granular in examining engagements could provide more information on the student's intentions to enroll at your institution.

Unfortunately, there's not currently a way to add meta data or associate a form to a mailing. And mirroring mailings with a dataset would be difficult and time-consuming to do. So some other options include

Filter: Maintain a list of these categorized emails to manually add as a filter

Folder: Create subfolders where these emails live to add as a filter

Name: Include a keyword like "Critical" in name of the emails that can have a formula filter written against them

Each of these require ongoing diligence to keep your mailings categorized and contributing to your model properly. A regular review and checklist for staff will help keep these requirements synced though.

Note from our Messenger Pigeon: Tailoring Calls to Actions to the student may increase the likelihood of the student engaging with your communications. A highly engaged local student is more likely to attend a Campus Tour than a full-need international student who may be more likely to attend a virtual event or Portal experience. Additional models to predict engagement topics can further refine your MarComms strategy.

Moments that Matter Behaviors: Application Anchors

Days from Event to App

Subquery Export

Dependent subquery

Formula ⌄

1   Row Limit

```
datediff(day,
@Form-Start-Date-Time,
@Application-Submitted-Date)
```

⊡ Export   ▪▪   Ț

Application Submitted Date

Form Start Date/Time

How students behave and engage around critical moments and milestones can have a substantial impact on their enrollment likelihood.

This example counts the number of days between an event and when the student submitted the application. This might pair better with assigning a value based on a close timeframe like within a week of the event.

Another indicator could be how long from when the application opened to when it was submitted. This starts to get into shakier territory as students applying for Early Decision/Action Rounds, or with better support/counseling, or certain demographic trends can introduce more noise than insights.

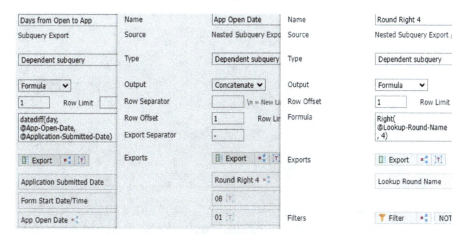

Another variable to explore would be how long from application submitted to completion. Again, there is likely to be considerable noise from populations that have additional requirements or constraints.

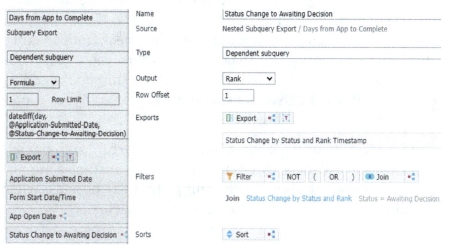

Moments that Matter Behaviors: Decision Anchors

Acritical glimpse into your student behaviors are how and if students engage around your outreach like admission decisions, financial aid awards, and transfer evaluations. Are they registering for events or reaching out to staff? Are they going radio silent? Are they filing appeals?

In this example, you calculate the time from the admission offer being opened to registering for an event. If that happens sometime between the day of opening and a week from opening, then that student gets a flag of '1'. Others get a '0'. While I harp on pre-decision behaviors a lot in this book, adding decision-anchored behaviors should be explored if your model incorporates that timeline.

Configurable Joins is such a robust, powerful, and flexible platform for feature engineering. The above examples are just a brief walk along some of the things that are possible when building these more complex and relational variables.

Conclusion

Effective feature engineering using time-anchored data enables institutions to build more accurate predictive models. By thoughtfully organizing and timestamping behaviors, institutions can capture the nuances of student engagement, leading to more informed decisions and better resource allocation. Through strategies like coalescing data, leveraging configurable joins, and creating multiple Models, we underscore the importance of tailoring Predictive Models to specific institutional goals, ultimately enhancing the student recruitment and enrollment process.

With you Engagement Scores and Predictive Models built, the stage has been set for the third act of our time together. Enter Adaptive Enrollment Management -

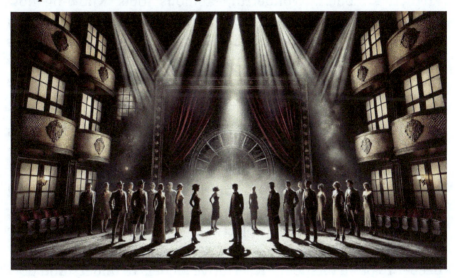

ACT III: ADAPTIVE ENROLLMENT MANAGEMENT

We've spent this book building Engagement Scores and Predictive Models. Wonderful, fabulous tools. Knowing how engaged your student is, and how they are interacting with you can be critical in understanding how their student journey is progressing. And digging through this layer to understand how that engagement is changing allows institutions to be proactive to keep students active and successful.

Understanding at any given moment how likely a student is to apply, enroll, drop out, graduate, donate, or engage in some other kind of modeled outcome opens an entire world of possibilities for your institution. It allows you to understand the student, broader populations, and the entire funnel. Between planning and projections to empowering strategic enrollment management, we can also go that additional layer deeper to build offshoot Prescriptive Models to understand how anticipated or nudged behaviors affect projections of things like headcounts, net tuition revenue, discount rate, etc.

Modeling also unlocks more strategic recruitment and programming, delivering the right action to the students, populations, and geographies that will benefit the most. This includes identifying outperforming schools and relationships that can be replicated elsewhere and untapped areas that could become high impact with just a bit of work and resources. It also extends into more strategic name acquisitions.

This deeper understanding also allows for far greater tailoring on marketing, communications, and the student journey. It helps prioritize high-touch and high-cost resources like calls, print, and person-centered interventions and programming that cannot be scaled to the entire funnel. And with a wide spectrum of explicit (told us on a form), inferred (Ping site tracking or vendor trend data), or projected (1st party correlations) interests for enrollment priorities like academics, financial aid, or post-graduation goals, this analytical framework can wrap around the students in a tailored, automated way that can truly differentiate your institutions from others.

What it leads to is a principle I've coined Adaptive Enrollment Management (AEM). It uses Strategic Enrollment Management to architecture the work and Artisanal Student Journeys driven by the deep understanding of the student (or probability thereof), some of which we're covering in this book as the three pillars. And while AEM is a topic for an entire book itself, it is a helpful way to focus Scoring and Modeling as a north star.

That's right! This book wasn't about the quest to build Engagement Scoring and predictive models at all. It was to improve the success and journey of your students and institution!

What a 3rd act twist. There is a light at the end of the tunnel. It just turns out to be a BEACON. But there's time enough to get into that in Act III of our time together.

The final series of chapters will cover how to use Scores and Models not only in an evaluatory and projective way, but also to implement proactive and prescriptive strategies. The use cases will be centered around Admission, Recruitment, and Enrollment, but the AEM framework is also highly applicable to Student Success and Advancement.

The use of Engagement Scores and Predictive Models in higher education continues to innovate and unlock the ways institutions approach strategic planning and enrollment management. The rest of this book will focus on some of these use cases.

I've created acronyms for each of the topics to help communicate and build the principles. As a sneak preview, here's what's to come in this, the final act:

TARGET Projections: **T**uition **A**id and **R**ecruitment **G**oals **E**stimation **T**ool. This Predictive Modeling strategy is tailored for admissions professionals. It projects individual student enrollment likelihood, incoming class sizes, anticipated net tuition revenue, discount rates, and remaining financial aid budgets. It Empowers you to make data-driven decisions, optimizing recruitment efforts and financial planning to achieve enrollment and revenue goals effectively. Paired with a reporting tool like Slate, current funnel statistics, institutional goals, projected totals, and even nudged projected totals can be viewed at the same time to craft incoming classes.

CRAFTing your Class: **C**ustomized **R**ecruitment **A**ctions using **F**orecasting and **T**argeting. This Predictive Modeling strategy helps craft and yield the incoming class by understanding individual student needs, tailoring outreach and programming, and prioritizing resources where they are most impactful. CRAFT leverages predictive insights to transform admissions from transactional to transformational.

NUDGE: **N**urturing **U**ser **D**ecisions with **G**uided **E**ngagement.

A prescriptive Modeling strategy that empowers institutions to proactively understand and influence student behaviors affecting enrollment likelihood, anticipated headcount, and net tuition revenue. This enables data-driven actions to achieve recruitment goals successfully. It also provides a framework to project how anticipated actions will affect student and class probabilities and counts.

BEACON Data Mining: **B**ehavioral and **E**cospherical **A**nalytics for **C**onversion **O**ptimization and **N**avigation. Using Slate-tracked engagement data and biodemographic data along with trends in their environment like 3rd-party trend and ACS data built into Slate to better understand students. This framework can be used to developed variables for Scoring and Modeling as well as to craft more meaningful and impactful MarComms and student experiences.

GPS Resource Allocation - **G**uided **P**rioritization **S**trategy. Using Scoring and Predictive Modeling to prioritize high cost and high touch resources like staff/faculty/student phone calls, tailored print mailings, and person-centered interventions for students with a higher likelihood to apply or enroll to make a larger impact and ROI on your efforts.

SCOUT Recruitment: **S**trategic **C**ommunity **O**utreach and **U**niversity **T**ravel. A recruitment strategy that focuses on identifying trends and forming strategies around recruitment efforts, including travel, building relationships, leveraging fit dynamics, and augmenting outreach to enhance engagement and boost enrollment outcomes.

THRIVE: **T**argeted **H**uman-centered **R**esources and **I**ntervention for **V**ital **E**mpowerment. A prescriptive Modeling strategy that empowers institutions to proactively deliver tailored programming that helps students succeed. By investing in recruitment and student success through customized support based on predictive analytics, THRIVE ensures students not only enroll but truly flourish at the university.

Bonus: **EnrollMentor:** The role of Modeling and generative AI will continue to expand for staff. Whether in understanding information, creating content, or offering recommendations, you're not building a tool. You are spinning up a staff member. A consultant, personal assistant, data scientist, and advisor. You're building an EnrollMentor, providing insight, strategy, and direction at every step of your processes. This book helps you leverage this EnrollMentor.

CHAPTER 12: TARGET - PROJECTIONS AND GOALS

TARGET Projections: **T**uition **A**id and **R**ecruitment **G**oals **E**stimation **T**ool. This Predictive Modeling strategy is tailored for admissions professionals. It projects individual student enrollment likelihood, incoming class sizes, anticipated net tuition revenue, discount rates, and remaining financial aid budgets. It Empowers you to make data-driven decisions, optimizing recruitment efforts and financial planning to achieve enrollment and revenue goals effectively. Paired with a reporting tool like Slate, current funnel statistics, institutional goals, projected totals, and even nudged projected totals can be viewed at the same time to craft incoming classes.

We'll focus predominantly on Predictive Modeling, but this is applicable to a lesser extent if your institution is limited to Engagement Scoring. If you have validated your Score against an outcome like applying or enrolling, then it may be a reasonable proxy for the Predictive Model in some cases. Prioritizing your work and strategizing in the context of a value, whether it's a Model or Score will help you move your institution forward.

Whether you want to know how likely a particular person is to perform a behavior (apply, enroll, engage with MarComms, drop out, be put on probation, graduate, donate, or some other use case), Modeling can also help in the aggregate of your populations. In other words, you get the forest AND the trees.

Planning And Projections

Planning

Metric	Prospects	Inquiry	Apps	Admitted	Enrolled
Total	2615	2125	1141	644	
Projected to Apply	656	609			
Projected to Enroll	150	150		91	

Net Tuition Revenue

Metric	Admitted	Enrolled
Institution		
Total	644	
Projected to Apply		
Projected to Enroll	91	
Projected NTR	$4,689,385	
Projected Aid Diff	$4,624,413	
Projected Discount Rate	48.7%	

By Major

Top 3	
Engineering	$376,233
Criminal Justice	$324,090
History	$328,533

Lowest 3	
Education	$29,003
Nursing	$92,133
Visual and Performing Arts	$78,755

Projected Incoming Class: By Major

Reporting Values Name	# Projected to Enroll in Majors	NTR $ Projected to Enroll in Majors	# Projected to Enroll with Weighted Nudged Behaviors in Majors	NTR $ Projected to Enroll with Weighted Nudged Behaviors in Majors
Biological Sciences	13	$775,624	17	$515,921
Computer Science	27	$803,984	18	$992,902
Education	35	$768,175	20	$840,281
Mechanical Engineering	14	$959,474	16	$1,041,283

Projected Incoming Class: All

All Students	# Projected to Enroll	NTR $ Projected to Enroll	# Projected to Enroll with Weighted Nudged Behaviors	NTR $ Projected to Enroll with Weighted Nudged Behaviors
All Students	437	$22,536,645	461	$24,315,901

Person-Level Projections

Ref ID	Percent Likely to Enroll	Percent Likely to Enroll With Weighted Nudge	Percent Likely to Enroll With Weighted Nudge x2	Major 1
116216007	92%	93%	94%	Education
342591879	92%	92%	94%	Education
379674066	91%	92%	93%	History
429483363	91%	92%	93%	History
387259432	91%	92%	93%	Education
376847930	84%	86%	87%	History
246439976	67%	68%	59%	History
384923240	64%	67%	70%	History
470014144	81%	84%	87%	Education
365516836	39%	42%	59%	History
794412390	53%	56%	52%	Mechanical Engineering
453603103	42%	45%	49%	History
502080473	39%	41%	44%	Mechanical Engineering

The first forest is planning. With application Modeling, you can examine the prospect pool to ballpark the number of applications you will receive and staff accordingly. The model will miss stealth applications, so these have to be planned for separately through your historical data. Though many of the principles in this book may lead you to gather these names before they have the opportunity to apply pre-Slate.

Similarly, with enrollment Modeling, an institution can match heads to beds, and paired with Financial Aid in Slate, model net tuition revenue, budgeted aid, discount rate, etc. throughout the process. These projections can also be applied to programs for planning and assessing needs and resources.

The pictured report gives you a zoomed out view of the institution and progression. With Likelihood to Apply and

Likelihood to Enroll models built into Slate (or with the results integrated into Slate), you can examine the size of your prospect pool to estimate the number of applications. With your admits (or at least tentative admits) coded, you can estimate the number of students that will enroll.

In this example, you have also added record-level net tuition revenue (NTR) - or calculated it from costs and any aid and scholarships for the students. Based on the Likelihood to Enroll model, this report calculates the anticipated NTR, Discount Rate, and anticipated aid spend. It also floats the top and bottom three programs based on anticipated NTR.

Additional comparisons Year-over-Year could also be presented to examine any trends or align with any historical benchmarks.

Goal Alignment And Tracking

Projected Incoming Class: By Major

Reporting Values Name	Records	Apps	Admits	Goal	# Projected to Enroll in Majors	NTR $ Projected to Enroll in Majors	# Projected to Enroll with Weighted Nudged Behaviors in Majors	NTR $ Projected to Enroll with Weighted Nudged Behaviors in Majors
In-State	188	98	65	45	43	$2,142,499	46	$2,309,948
International	181	66	38	32	28	$1,321,623	30	$1,445,160
Low GPA	283	142	82	55	60	$3,007,940	65	$3,254,372
Other	1346	729	459	75	322	$16,064,583	347	$17,306,329

Slate becomes an even more valuable reporting resource when institutional goals are added directly to Slate. This report tracks live data - the number of prospects/inquiries, applicants, and admits. It also tracks the "goal" number of enrolling students. We'll discuss how this is done shortly. It then projects the number of students likely to enroll (and their associated NTR) as well as an augmented version of the projection. These can be the anticipated cycle changes and/or prescriptive nudges (more on that in the NUDGE chapter).

As seen in this example, the projected number of students is not matching with your goals.

In-State students	International students	Low GPA group
Admitted: 65 Goal: 45 Projected: 43 Need: 2 additional students	Admitted: 38 Goal: 32 Projected: 28 Need: 4 additional students	Admitted: 82 Goal: 55 Projected: 60 Need: 5 fewer students

Before we go further, let's pause to build this report. The Base for this data table Query is actually a Dataset I created and called Reporting Values. I use this methodology across several projects to get more flexible reports. I initially developed it to strategically monitor course scheduling, registration behaviors, and success metrics, but it found a great use for this kind of dynamic stitching of report elements.

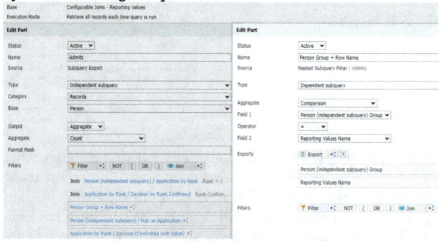

The name of the Dataset record establishes the row name and is correlated with a field value (or dynamic criteria from the students through an Existence export) like In-State or International.

The live data columns from your funnel are pulled through a series of Independent Subqueries. A filter pulls the relevant students to the name of the row.

The Goal values (number of students, NTR, etc. are added as fields on the Dataset as seen in the below picture. The projected number of students can be calculated by using the Slate fields automated in the earlier process in this book or by calculating the values live in the report. We will go through this second process in the NUDGE chapter along with augmented projections as well.

Internal Use

As you project the number of applicants and enrolling students, this also helps plan internally. When was the last time you had the same number of applications in back-to-back years? Modeling can help determine how many part-time readers you'll need to hire. And how angry was Housing last time you overenrolled the number of students? How about Financial Aid when you overspent aid. Or your CFO when your NTR or discount rate wasn't what they called "right".

While we'll work on CRAFTing your class in the next chapter, there are a variety of internal uses for Scores and Models. And with the data in Slate, they're easy to plug and use them anywhere.

The information is also helpful in the Reader Review Form. This can be as a Merge Field added to an Instructions block

Automated Score as embedded Merge Fields

Automated Score:
Raw Score: {{Total-Engagement-Score}}
Translated: {{Total-Engagement-Score-Translation-Code}}

Adding a translated version of the Score can help accommodate the part of the application cycle the staff is reading at. While reading an app in August versus February might have different total numbers, seeing it in context of the broader pool will help keep reading a bit more consistent. Though the trends in typical time of engagement for population varies, this tool helps normalize it and aggregate the datapoints of a typically slow process, allowing staff to prioritize other information instead of counting events and Interactions.

If the staff member does their own formal evaluation of interest, this automated Score does not necessarily replace that staff score. After all, there is likely additional information and factors that are not included in the automated Score. But the two will most certainly be highly correlated. Keeping it close at hand to help staff can provide information at a glance that may have required an in-depth review and considerations otherwise.

It can even be used to prefill that staff score. Separate fields should be used here though. The process we built to automate the Score will automatically update the field and overwrite the manually updated staff score. This pictured example uses the staff field and with a default formula, Slate simply adds the automated Scores (translated from 100-pt to a 5-pt scale). If the staff feels the automated Score is accurate, they can move on. Alternatively, they can update it. Because this prefilled value may anchor staff to that value, the Scoring rubric should be validated before using it in this way.

Application Review: Demonstrated Interest

*Automated Score is pre-filled. Update as needed

☐ Hide Label

Placeholder Text	
System Field	Application Fields ⌄ · App: Score - Sample App E\
Null Handling	☐ Enable custom null handling
Export Key	sys:app:sample_app_eval_di
Data Type	Text/Unspecified ⌄
Size	Width: 48
Format Mask	
Maximum Counts	Characters: · Words: · Display: D
Minimum Counts	Characters: · Words: · Display: D
Calculation Formula	
Auto-suggest	⌄
Default Value Formula	☑
Exports	⊞ Export · ⸬ ⸬ · ◐ Join · ⸬

Join Application

Join Application / Person

Total-Engagement-Score-1-5-Translation-Code

Formula   @Total-Engagement-Score-1-5-Translation-Code

Because the automated Score is highly correlated with the staff evaluations, that also makes it ideal for training new staff though. This real-time context on new files can help guide them as they learn more and become comfortable with the process while decreasing the time spent re-evaluating applications from a previous cycle.

Forensic Enrollment Management

At the time of writing this book, a new concept is about to be released into the wild at AACRAO SEM called Forensic

Enrollment Management.

I was skimming an email about the conference when I saw it for the first time. I had already been developing my Adaptive Enrollment Management framework but struggling to communicate it. It was built on top of three fundamental legs - SEM, data mining, and artisanal MarComms and experiences.

This email came in about 20 minutes before a job interview.

Introducing FEM: Forensic Enrollment Management to Unlock Institutional Revenue

FEM is an intentional redirection away from targeting headcount and toward maximizing revenue. Learn to unlock the revenue and inform decision-making in a sustainable way.

Intrigued by the email, I asked ChatGPT to explain FEM and how it differed from SEM. I hadn't heard of the concept before but if it helped me explain AEM in my interview a few minutes away, I wanted a quick intake.

ChatGPT essentially described FEM as BEACON data mining.

It was such a wonderful coincidence. My father spent a large portion of his career as a Forensic Investigator. You may be aware of the job from shows like CSI, a show he consulted and had his cases used in. And I was vaguely aware of forensic accounting as a method to track the flow of specific money. Investigative data mining was exactly what AEM was built off of.

I was surprised I hadn't heard of it before. And it was such a comforting discovery. Less than two weeks before this email, my father had passed away on August 7th, 2024.

A few minutes later, I joined the interview for the next few hours and mentioned FEM as I described the work I was doing with

AEM. It wasn't until after the interview that I started googling FEM to learn more about it.

And what do you know? It wasn't a thing.

FEM was a concept being unveiled at AACRAO SEM that focused on NTR in the enrollment process.

While I look forward to learning more about FEM as it relates heavily to everything in this and in future books I am planning on writing, I am absolutely crushed that I missed being able to build the Forensic Enrollment Management concept from the ground up in a way to honor and remember my father.

He would have gotten such a kick out of continuing the principles of his work in my own. But even without the name, the principles are there. And will be with everyone who learns from this book and implements them into their own work. And everyone who does use Forensic Enrollment Management will also carry on a bit of the legacy and impact he left on this world that inspired that new concept as well.

Conclusion

Embracing Predictive Modeling tools like TARGET Projections empowers you to make informed, strategic decisions that align with your enrollment objectives and financial requirements.

By projecting both individual behaviors and aggregate trends, your admission team gains valuable insights that enhance recruitment efforts and internal planning. Whether utilizing sophisticated Models or Engagement Scoring, incorporating these data-driven approaches facilitates goal alignment and progress tracking. Ultimately, this empowers you to prioritize effectively, navigate challenges, and advance your institution's mission in an increasingly competitive educational environment.

CHAPTER 13: CRAFTING YOUR CLASS

CRAFTing your Class: **C**ustomized **R**ecruitment **A**ctions using **F**orecasting and **T**argeting. This Predictive Modeling strategy helps craft and yield the incoming class by understanding individual student needs, tailoring outreach and programming, and prioritizing resources where they are most impactful. CRAFT leverages predictive insights to transform admissions from transactional to transformational.

Guiding Strategy

Let's begin to elaborate on this data and see how you can start taking actions from it to craft your incoming class. We'll do this in an Excel version to explain some particular use cases for your Predictive Modeling results. Modeling can guide your institutional practice in these moments. It can be leveraged in strategic recruitment to help

Class Building							High Yield: In-State			
Groups	Admits	Goal		Projected			Count	ID	Phone Number	Yield %
		Yield	Count	Yield	Count	Effort				
In-State	65	69%	45	66%	43	2	1	000026	111-1136	91%
Internatio	38	84%	32	74%	28	4	2	000030	111-1140	94%
Low GPA	82	67%	55	73%	60	-5	3	000032	111-1142	92%
Other	100	40%	40	30%	30	10	4	000033	111-1143	91%
Total	285	60%	172	56%	161	11	5	000034	111-1144	91%

- Craft the class
  - You expect too many students from one of your groups
    - Automatically email them the option to take a Gap Year
- Offer tailored support and programming for populations that need it,
  - Identified Low GPA students who
    - Have low real yield or low projected yield based on a tailored model
    - But higher projected yield based on more general models
    - Identifying pain points in enrollment management
  - Create an Academic Preparedness Workshop to help yield, retention, and student success for these under-enrolling or under-retained students
- Prioritize human action and other high resources interventions where it's needed most to meet Goals.

- You need 20 more students from one of your groups

    - Excel and Slate can automatically generate a list of high-yield students for high-touch efforts like phone calls

Generating Lists

Let's take a look at how Excel is doing this before moving on.

Column I contains static numbers, increasing 1 at a time. Columns J-L merge in data from the tab containing student data "Modeling Projections" in this case. I use Index/Matching but VLOOKUP is a popular alternative.*

Note: Even the resident Report Ghost Writer is not sure why VLOOKUP is popular. She still supports YOUR decision to use it though!

```
=COUNTIFS(
AG$7:AG31,
">" & 0.9)
```

M	AG
Likely to Enroll > 90%	Probability
AG31,	27%
1	91%
1	38%
1	42%
1	67%
2	94%
2	61%
3	92%
4	91%

The trick to automating the list is creating the sequential numbers in your data tab. Column M is counting the number of times a Score greater than .9 (90%) is seen in a range. That range is specified as AG$7 to AG31. "AG$7" refers to the first row with data, and the "$7" keeps the reference locked to that cell as the formula is repeated on every row in Column M. "AG31" is the current row of the formula, so the formula counts the number of times .9 is seen from the start of the data to the current row.

That creates a sequential column where the first time a number is seen by the Index/Match is the next time a record meets the criteria of greater than 90%.

This may be an underwhelming use case for the process, but I developed it in a separate project for an SIS implementation. While switching from Banner to Workday, GPAs and Units were not matching in the new system. Some classes too weren't on the new records, so I needed to generate recurring lists of all affected records by their specific error. One tab listed all students with missing courses (along with the name, credits, and term of the course). Another tab listed students with a different GPA, different number of Units, but with no missing classes (along with the respective data points from both systems). With several other tabs listing students by various specific errors.

I had initially planned to write a macro to do the listing, but even that was far too cumbersome, so this autolist process where I added new data and the lists refreshed was a game-changer for investigating and resolving issues both through individual corrections and system updates based on the lists.

But I digress. The Slate version of this prioritization list is far simpler. In your Report or Query, restrict your Query to just students that meet your criteria. The pictured example will list students with an Engagement Score greater than or equal to 3 by using a Comparison Subquery Filter.

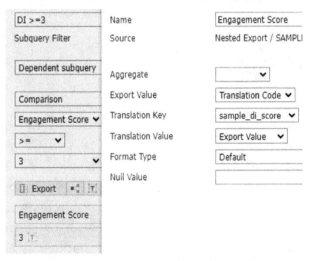

Another feature of this Filter is the use of a Translation Code on the Engagement Score. It converts the raw 100-pt scale into a data-specific classification of engagement. You may want to prioritize a program or outreach to your highly engaged students, but what number do you use in August? That's probably not the same number in February? This Translation Code Excel update looks at the percentiles of your current records to create Score bands. It's quick and easy to update from

Slate data and re-upload to update the Translation Code.

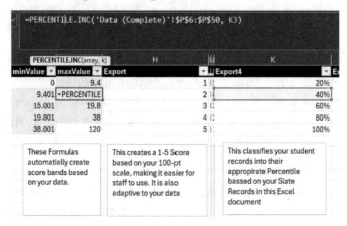

=PERCENTILE.INC('Data (Complete)'!$P$6:$P$50, K3)				

These Formulas automatially create score bands based on your data.

This creates a 1-5 Score based on your 100-pt scale, making it easier for staff to use. It is also adaptive to your data

This classifies your student records into their appropirate Percentile bassed on your Slate Records in this Excel document

Intervention Validation

Post-Experiment: In-State			
Groups	**Admits**	**Yield**	**Enrolled**
In-State	65	69%	45
- Experiment Group	20	80%	16
- Received Phone Call	10	90%	9
- No Call (Control)	10	70%	7
- Other Students	45	64%	29

With a baseline application or yield expectation, Predictive Modeling allows you to "test" the effects of new policies and practices. Instead of using a propensity score match or some kind of randomized study, this will be a more attainable way to measure how effective a new yield plan or application nudge was at getting your students to act. It does require a highly accurate model to use as that baseline comparison though or at least to create treatment and control groups.

In this example, your 65 In-State admits needed an intervention to increase the number of yielding students to meet your institutional goals. Twenty high-yield likelihood students were chosen for the investigation. Ten would receive a phone call and ten more would serve as a control group who did not receive this new intervention. Each group was expected to yield about 7 students.

After the call, that group yielded two additional students, bringing their anticipated yield up from 70% to an actual yield of 90%. If all twenty students would have received the call, you may have come close to getting those five additional students you needed from the group.

But now that you have piloted this new practice and validated it with a similar control group, you can more strategically deploy your resources next year to the broader group as needed.

Similar to the previous situations, this can be tracked in Slate provided the intervention itself is tracked in Slate or some other flag to track the intervention on the students is used.

Diverging Models

Let's review another interesting use case in Excel. We can use the auto-generated lists again to identify students who have diverging predicted yield based on the multiple models (e.g. International Model versus the Financial Aid Yes Model). The pictured example shows an international admit applying for financial aid whose yield is predicted at 80% likely based on the data and behaviors determined to be predictive for International students. Based on the data and behaviors determined to be predictive for financial aid students, they are only 30% likely to enroll.

This allows you to tailor outreach, programming, and assistance that speaks to their experience as a student with financial need as opposed to just the aspects associated with their international student experience.

There could also be a trend with these students. Could some other data or interaction be added to the models that more accurately captures the experience and outcomes for these students? Or perhaps a new model could be spun up and added to their aggregated predictive Scores.

In this situation:

Model Inconsistencies								
Model ID	Intl				FINA Y			
	Academics	Need	Attendance	Yield	Academic	Need	Logins	Yield
000013	4	4	2	80%	4	4	0	30%
Effect	Positive	Positive	Positive		Positive	Negative	Positive	

Academics. the Academic variable is positively associated with enrollment likelihood in both models (i.e. is the number goes up, the % likely also goes up)

Need. This variable has a different relationship to enrollment likelihood between the models. International admits are more likely to enroll the higher their need. Students on aid more generally though are less likely to enroll the more need they have.

Attendance. This variable was only used in your International model. It counts the number of events the student attended. As the number goes up, the likelihood to enroll goes up.

Logins. This variable was only used in your Financial Aid Yes model. It counts the number of times the student logged into their portal. Again, as this number goes up, the likelihood to enroll goes up.

While this student visited campus multiple times, they are not as virtually engaged leading to some of the difference in yield likelihood. For the Need variable, perhaps aid is more competitive for international admits or they are typically receiving additional grants or funding than domestic admits. Or your institution is still a strong choice for high-need international students. Alternatively, no and low-need international admits may have other options that they tend to enroll at. Students on aid might have a larger number of domestic students or the negative correlation is more pronounced, pulling the relationship with them from their smaller international counterparts. This could be masking International student's true likelihood to enroll under the guide of need's relationship to enrollment of a different group. It could even be that Need is positively correlated with yield, but it's being hidden by sub groups having distinctly different likelihoods to enroll (Simpson's Paradox).

Understanding these contrasts and trends in these models can shed light on shortcomings, contradictions, and sub populations. Maybe some kind of additional support is needed on the institution side that could address the broader population that hasn't been identified yet. Perhaps that is automated or perhaps it will be more resource-intensive, but this nuance can drive significant and meaningful work that will improve student and institutional success.

Whatever the underlying reason for these divergences, this investigation is an important element in driving impactful outcomes.

Let's look at this from the person level.

- This record has a 80% likelihood to enroll (or to be retained, donate, etc.).

- What does the institution need to do to support them?

- What are the predictors or other data that can guide programming or outreach for this student?

- How do they deviate from enrolling students with a similar likelihood to enroll?

- The student's academics and financial need aren't going to change. They probably also won't attend another event given they are international and already attended twice. But CTAs related to virtual events, their portal, and other forms of engagement may be the next most impactful strategy given their Aid Model persona.

- What about other high-need, academically strong international admits who have visited campus? Perhaps Admitted student questionnaires or available interviews with current and former students within that persona can inform you what made them decide to attend (or not attend).

- Perhaps the student wants to create a new, financially-stable life in your country? Vignettes about successful international students might highlight the value of your institution. Or they are concerned about finding a community on your campus, so highlighting affinity groups and cultural hubs that are available to them can be the selling point that convinces them to enroll.

There are many strategies that could nudge this student who

is already likely to enroll but might be missing some critical element to ensure their interest in your institution.

You may need to move the needle in enrollment. Trying to herd a 1,000 cats with 10,000 motivations just is not feasible. These likelihood values allow you to focus more time and resources where it's needed most and will have the greatest impact. Both at the person level but also a handful of crafted personas that the above messaging can be prioritized for. And if you build three of these personas every year, automating the outreach for them, in five years, you could have fifteen, likely encompassing hundreds of students that have these artisanal student experiences curated for them.

Your institution does not need more transactional interactions with your students. They need transformational strategies where the staff, students, faculty, and even the communications and virtual experience know the prospective students that they are engaging with. Engagement can build on that knowledge to truly see and work with them to be successful. This meaningful relationship allows for exchanges to be relevant, timely, and impactful.

Financial Aid Optimization

Another important element of not only crafting the class but making college accessible and increasing student success is financial aid optimization.

There is also the market reality that institutions find themselves in. One that will continue to get harsher. Between demographic and search cliffs, decreased perceptions around higher education, and even external competition, a dropping tide lowers all ships.

The following chapters will navigate several ways to increase the likelihood of a student to apply and enroll at your institution, but I do want to mention how Predictive Modeling can be used to manage financial resources efficiently. Understanding what amount of aid will likely lead to an enrollment while not over distributing allows you to not only attract students but maintain a healthy budget to create an incoming class that brings together every slice of the community.

This process can become even more complex when you start using more feature engineering on your data. Two families that receive the same amount of aid may still have different struggles with paying the remaining balance. As those contextual pieces around how much reach is still required to pay for college, you can get a better idea than just giving another 5k to a group of students already getting 20k in aid.

This contextual data built into the Modeling not only helps deliver the optimal amount of aid, but it can be valuable in accurately predicting likelihood to enroll. Adding a feedback loop to help identity stretch needs from enrolling and non-enrolling (especially paired with an Admitted Student Questionnaire) can continue to finetune how well you can identify, predict, and intervene.

The Nudge chapter will show practical and technical examples of how you can program changes in your model like the amount of aid given. These theoretical changes can be seen side by side or in iterations to see how the changes impact the likelihood of not only a single student to enroll but the broader number of incoming students, NTR, and remaining financial aid.

This can be done both in a tool like Excel but also directly in Slate. Instead of seeing how an additional campus tour would affect enrollment likelihood, you're adding money to their aid package.

This process allows you to enroll the students your institution needs, optimize the NTR, and strategically deploy aid dollars.

As a caveat, your competitors are also trying to fill their incoming class. And with fewer students, advances in technology, and a changing financial aid landscape, current and future classes are likely to be more difficult than previous classes as your peers also go harder for the same students with fewer professional standards and guidelines. Students are also applying and depositing to more schools than ever before, keeping their options open until the very last moment. That means Predictive Modeling built on historical data may be less reliable at predicting future classes as the population, environment, and the context the new students are operating in are different.

Conclusion

If you are using Predictive Modeling to help CRAFT your class, these data-driven Scoring and Modeling techniques can help keep you informed and drive the strategy your institution needs to not only achieve institutional success but also student success.

Understanding your students helps align their interests and needs with the institution's. And you can make informed decisions that meet your institutional priorities, needs, and financial sustainability. With better enrollment, lower attrition, efficient resource allocation, you not only position your institution for success, but you can help CRAFT the next generation of students.

CHAPTER 14: PRESCRIPTIVE MODELING

NUDGE: Nurturing **U**ser **D**ecisions with **G**uided **E**ngagement. A prescriptive Modeling strategy that empowers institutions to proactively understand and influence student behaviors affecting enrollment likelihood, anticipated headcount, and net tuition revenue. This enables data-driven actions to achieve recruitment goals successfully. It also provides a framework to project how anticipated actions will affect student and class probabilities and counts.

Prescriptive Modeling is one of the most important benefits from using a model/algorithm that is easily explainable and replicable. In the previous chapter, we looked at how we can act on our Model projections to craft the class. In this chapter, we'll actually reprogram the model to see how your institutional actions or anticipated behaviors from the students can affect individual students and the incoming class as a whole.

This allows you to not only get more passive information but to actually understand what steps you need to SUCCESSFULLY push the boulder up the hill. Year after year. Cycle after cycle. Student after student.

Augmenting Models In Slate

Projected Incoming Class: By Major

Reporting Values Name	Records	Apps	Admits	Goal	# Projected to Enroll in Majors	NTR $ Projected to Enroll in Majors	# Projected to Enroll with Weighted Nudged Behaviors in Majors	NTR $ Projected to Enroll with Weighted Nudged Behaviors in Majors
In-State	188	98	65	45	43	$2,142,499	46	$2,309,948
International	181	66	38	32	28	$1,321,623	30	$1,445,160
Low GPA	283	142	82	55	60	$3,007,940	65	$3,254,372

Your institution has given you a series of goals for your incoming class. Perhaps it is headcount, NTR, and discount rate. Perhaps there are subgoals for the makeup of your class. A certain number of students from your state or international or in STEM majors. Perchance, the goals change every two weeks.

Slate Reports can show updated and live views not just of your projected headcount, NTR, etc., but also how those projections might change. These changes can be thought of as anticipated cycle changes and prescriptive nudges.

Projected Incoming Class: By Major

Reporting Values Name	# Projected to Enroll in Majors	NTR $ Projected to Enroll in Majors	# Projected to Enroll with Weighted Nudged Behaviors in Majors	NTR $ Projected to Enroll with Weighted Nudged Behaviors in Majors
Biological Sciences	15	$570,634	17	$615,921
Biology	23	$1,264,673	24	$1,350,074
Business	20	$492,177	22	$528,576

Projected Incoming Class: All

All Students	# Projected to Enroll	NTR $ Projected to Enroll	# Projected to Enroll with Weighted Nudged Behaviors	NTR $ Projected to Enroll with Weighted Nudged Behaviors
All Students	457	$22,536,645	493	$24,315,809

Person-Level Projections

Ref ID	Percent Likely to Enroll	Percent Likely to Enroll With Weighted Nudge	Percent Likely to Enroll With Weighted Nudge v2	Major 1
846939606	67%	69%	69%	History
064923340	64%	67%	70%	History
104614144	61%	64%	67%	Education
305301836	59%	62%	65%	History
748421250	55%	58%	62%	Mechanical Engineering
852932163	42%	45%	49%	History
902680475	38%	41%	44%	Mechanical Engineering

Anticipated Cycle Changes

By examining previous cycles, you know roughly how behaviors in the model are likely to change throughout the rest of the cycle. For example, based on historical data, 30% of your admits will attend your Admitted Student day, 75% will spend 2 more hours on your website, and 5% will click on a link in an email, etc.

In this screenshot you can modify the live behavior counts tracked in Slate to change the Logit calculation by a weighted nudge amount. In excel, you can randomly apply a change in behavior (add an event attendance, additional Ping data, etc.) since you can quickly and easily write row-specific formulas. In a Slate Report, you have to apply a weighted nudge, so you are applying a % of the behavior change equivalent to the % you expect to perform the behaviors.

In particular, you expect 15% of students to get 5 additional points in your 100-pt behavior by the Commit Deadline. Since you can't randomly assign values to each record in the Slate Report, you add .75 points (5pt x 15%) to every record. For more refined results, you could upload the 5-pt bump into Slate for select records, or incorporate a Model to predict the likelihood of students to receive these increases. If you are doing that much work and going out of system anyways, you may prefer to just work with the data in Excel for the added flexibility it provides.

The report shows in additional columns anticipated student-level probabilities to enroll with these anticipated behaviors as well as new expected incoming class data like headcounts and NTR. I will explain each pop-up below from the first to last level.

You should read them first to last and last to first both to best understand the process and steps, especially if you're not as familiar with Configurable Joins. We're heading off the edge of the map, mate. Here there be monsters

Export Pop-Up 1: Independent Subquery - Using the Aggregate function to Sum the number of anticipated incoming students. This is done by either adding the % they are likely to enroll (Student A is 65% likely to enroll, Student B is 75% likely to enroll, Student C is 60% likely to enroll, adding to 200% or 2 students likely to enroll in the aggregate), adding student predicted to enroll (every student with >=50% likely to enroll gets codes as 1 incoming student, <50% likely to enroll gets coded as 0 incoming students), etc.

Export Pop-Up 2: Dependent Subquery - This Formula can be used to segment the record as projected to enroll and/or as a safety check to keep within 0-100%.

Export Pop-Up 3: Dependent Subquery - This Formula takes the logit (predictive model results) and converts it into a 0-100% likely to enroll. 2.718... is Euler's number. It is the base for natural logarithms similar to pi in that the numbers goes on forever without repeating. This formula takes 2.718... and raises it to the power of the logit before dividing it by 1 plus the same number.

Export Pop-Up 4: Dependent Subquery - This applies the predictive model to the student data.

Export Pop-Up 5: Dependent Subquery - This Formula keeps the individual behaviors being modified within 0 and the specified limit.

Export Pop-Up 6: Dependent Subquery - This Formula takes the student's behavior and adds the nudge or anticipate cycle action.

Export Pop-Up 7: Dependent Subquery - This formula calculates the size of the nudge/anticipated action. In this case you take the size of the nudge and are weighting it to the % of students you anticipate would have taken it. If you had another model predicting how likely the student would be to take it, you can add that Modeling here as well.

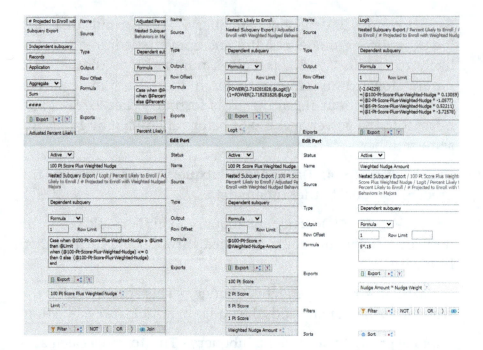

Prescriptive Nudges

Let's examine the Excel version of this process with the Prescriptive* lens, though Anticipated Cycle actions and Prescriptive nudges can be programmed into Slate reports or Excel in similar same ways.

Note from the Field of Statistics Mouse: Prescriptive models build on predictive insights to guide decisions. You can optimize decision-making by aligning institutional actions to meet established goals. Predictive models forecast future outcomes based on historical data, but they do not provide actionable recommendations.

Behaviors	Current		Augmented		Augmented (specified %) % of Recs 63%	
	Model	Projected	Adt. Pts	Projected	Adt. Pts	Projected
5 Pt Score	0.52211	17	1	20	3	20
5 Pt Score (Raw)	5 Pt Score (Raw)	Probability	5 Pt Score	Probability	5 Pt Score (Weighted)	Probability
4	2.08844	68%	2.61055	78%	2.61055	78%
3	1.56633	7%	2.08844	11%	2.61055	18%
4	2.08844	27%	2.61055	38%	2.08844	27%
4	2.08844	11%	2.61055	18%	2.61055	18%

In this screenshot, out of the 38 test records, you project 17 to matriculate. Let's look at a couple ways to calculate nudges to the 5-pt behavior in Excel -

When 1 pt is added to all records, expected matriculations increase to 20.

When 3 pts are added to a random ~70% of records, expected matriculations also increase to 20.

There is a maximum of 5 pts still enforced. The formulas in Excel and Slate are written to not exceed the total possible number of points specified for that behavior.

In the first example, a row-level formula compares if the student's behavior count plus the nudged amount (1 in this case) exceeds the limit. If so, then display the limit, otherwise show the sum of the two numbers.

This is a blunt method. You likely won't be able to affect behaviors for all students. I would recommend using the same weighted behavior shown in the Slate Report above in that case - add .75 points (5pt x 15%) to every record to approximate 15%

of your students getting a 5-point bump).

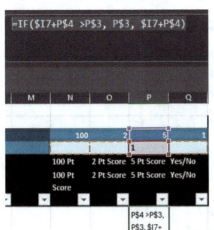

A more refined method would be applying the full behavior nudge to an expected percent of your records. In this case, you expect 70% of your students to change by 3 points.

The 70% in cell X4 assigned the % cutoff criteria. Row-level formulas in column X for each record creates a random number between 0 and 100 to evaluate against that criteria to decide if that record. Column W then checks for that flag to add the nudge. If so, it adds the nudged behaviors with the limit still imposed.

You may have a better idea than random on who will react to the nudge or anticipated cycle change. Maybe a model to predict the behaviors, registrations, or some other metric or weighting that would be more informative than a random assignment.

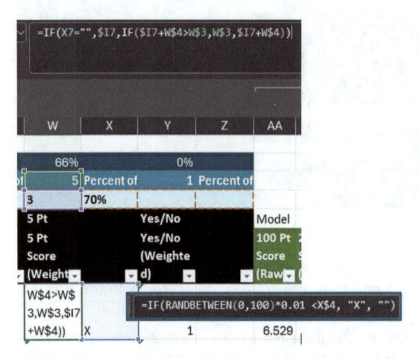

One last note with this method, you are assigning each student a flag based on the 70% cutoff criteria, but you should still confirm that the bonus is being applied to an appropriate number of students. Cell W2 divides the number of nudged students by the total number of students to determine what percent of records are actually getting the nudge. Over a larger group of students, this should be close, but a check cell is helpful.

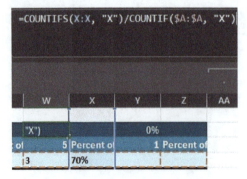

When you look at how these nudges affect your students and the group totals, you can examine current projections, the nudges to all, and the randomly assigned nudges quickly and easily in Excel.

Behaviors	Current			Augmented		Augmented (specified %)	
						% of Recs 63%	
	Model	Projected	Adt. Pts	Projected	Adt. Pts		Projected
5 Pt Score	0.52211	17	1	20	3		20
5 Pt Score (Raw)	5 Pt Score (Raw)	Probability	5 Pt Score	Probability	5 Pt Score (Weighted)		Probability
4	2.08844	68%	2.61055	78%	2.61055		78%
3	1.56633	7%	2.08844	11%	2.61055		18%
4	2.08844	27%	2.61055	38%	2.08844		27%
4	2.08844	11%	2.61055	18%	2.61055		18%

Let's examine your student-level data in this screenshot. That first student who scored a 4 out of 5 received the nudge, increasing enrollment likelihood by 10% across both scenarios since they could only increase by 1 point.

The second student (3 out of 5) increased their likelihood to enroll by 4 percent with 1 additional point and 11 percent because they could increase by 2 points before hitting the maximum allowed.

The forth student increased likelihood to enroll by 7 percent with 1 point added. They were not one of the 66% to have 3 points added, so in that scenario, their likelihood to matriculate is the same as the live data.

So if you can get all records to score 1 point higher or about seventy percent of their pool to score 3 points higher, then they can increase their matriculations by 3 people.

Because of the ease and speed to make hypothetical changes to these behaviors and see projections, especially in Excel, you can begin to craft strategic nudges, initiatives, and programming in real time that will help you meet your goals and increase student success. This also extends to financial aid optimization. Instead of increasing a student's event attendance, you're changing the aid amount to see their new likelihood to enroll. And as you provide financial nudges to individuals or groups, Slate and Excel will update the total expected incoming class, NTR, etc. dynamically and without having to go back and forth with a vendor or system.

Considerations

These are relatively general projection augmentations though, so this is more guidance unless these nudged behaviors have the same relationship as naturally occurring behaviors observed in the training data.

A good example of how these behaviors are contextual -

- An applicant spending 30 minutes on your Applicant Requirements page of your website
  - You expect them to be ~4% more likely to enroll after this behavior. *
  - To increase the total number of enrolling students, you:
    - Send an email to your admitted students with a CTA to read that web page.
  - That is not going to have the same effect on the likelihood to matriculate.
  - They are admitted students. Reading application requirements is not the same for them as it was for an applicant. They're not going to go the page, and even if they did, it's not going to change their enrollment behavior.

This is an over-the-top example, but it does illustrate how behaviors performed naturally vs nudged or at a certain time in the cycle or in relation to events will all have different relationships with enrollment likelihood. Some of this context can be coded into the model to better predict future records but others have to be understood when crafting these nudges.

Note from the Field of Statistics Mouse: **David used ~4% as a placeholder value. Consider three students with initial enrollment probabilities of 7%, 55%, and 91%. When they each receive the same increase in an independent variable (for example, an increase of 1 unit), they do not all experience the same absolute increase in their likelihood to enroll—neither personally nor statistically. This is because, in binary logistic regression, the effect of an independent variable is on the log-odds of the outcome, not directly on the probability. Although all students received the same "nudge," the impact on their enrollment probability is contextual and depends on their initial likelihood.**

- **Student A moves from a 7% to an 11% likelihood to enroll.**

- **Student B moves from a 55% to a 67% likelihood to enroll.**

- **Student C moves from a 91% to a 94% likelihood to enroll.**

Live Probability	Nudged Probability
7%	11%
55%	67%
91%	94%

The relationships, values, and defined levers can inform strategy though as we examine expected changes in outcomes. For example:

- The institution needs 15 more matriculants than being estimated

- The Modeling indicates that an event-related email will increase event attendance by about 3%.

- Attending that event would increase matriculation likelihood by about 5% on average

- So sending an additional email to 10,000 student may get 300 more event attendees

- 300 more event attendees may get 15 more matriculations

This example is a bit more of a stretch. It would require multiple Models running (Likelihood to attend an event, Likelihood to matriculate). The models are also probably looking more generally at emails and events, so adding a new email and specific event to the workstream may not have the same effects as the model indicates as seen in the first example.

Chaining multiple Models may compound any shortcomings in their makeup. Take the above situation if the nudges produced slightly different outcomes:

The institution needs 15 more matriculants than being

estimated

- Emailing our records only increased event attendance by 2%

- Attending this particular event only increased matriculation likelihood by 3%

- So sending the email to 10,000 student only got 200 more event attendees

- 200 more event attendees only got 6 more matriculations when the institution planned on 9 more than that based strictly on the models.

Conclusion

These examples do illustrate the systematic nature of binary logistic regression but also its limitations. Hopefully it sparks ideas on some out-of-the-box uses for it.

Predictive Modeling can become a crucial tool institutions leverage through the journey. And the fact that Slate can automatically update the likelihood of the outcomes based on augmented behaviors, many of the above actions can be automated and require little to no human intervention. That frees staff from the routine work to truly engage the students in human ways.

This becomes exponentially more powerful when you can prioritize the large impact behaviors and nudges that will most move the needle, something you know and can prescriptively implement because of your Modeling.

CHAPTER 15: BEACON - MARKETING AND COMMUNICATIONS

BEACON Data Mining: **B**ehavioral and **E**cospherical **A**nalytics for **C**onversion **O**ptimization and **N**avigation. Using Slate-tracked engagement data and biodemographic data along with trends in their environment like 3rd-party trend and ACS data built into Slate to better understand students. This framework can be used to developed variables for Scoring and Modeling as well as to craft more meaningful and impactful MarComms and student experiences. This was the investigative data mining that I thought Forensic Enrollment Management would be from that AACRAO Email. Don't remember that story from the TARGET Projections chapter? Let me remind you what I looked like AFTER talking about this non-existent concept at an interview for four hours -

But alas, the concepts, principles, and approaches became BEACON Data Mining. Since we already built our Scores and Models, we'll use BEACON as a framework to better understand your students and craft MarComms and experiences for them.

There are several ways to begin integrating Engagement Scoring and Predictive Modeling into your marketing and communications efforts. This includes:

- Triggering automated communications
- Augmenting the content of the communications
- Crafting personas and strategies
- Helping guide and prioritize high-resource outreach like print, voice, and human interaction.

Automated Communications

Understanding the level of engagement and the likelihood to apply or enroll can help in automated communications, even more so when paired with other Slate data or when Modeling on likelihood to engage with certain types of communications.

Highly engaged students, especially with a MarComm Subscore are eager to receive more communications from your institutions. This usually extends to students likely to enroll, but admitted student and applicant questionnaires can also help understand if enrolling and non-enrolling students generally want more communications from you. If they want less, it could mean you send too much or that the content wasn't engaging the student enough to want to read your emails.

But given the number of emails, texts, and print students receive from all of the institutions that have their name, focusing your communications becomes more important, and holding some in reserve specifically for students who want to engage with them or piloting communications to those more receptive to them can be an effective way to leverage Scoring and Modeling into your automated and drip communications. This can be especially true for very high likelihood students receiving a nudge to keep the institution at the top of mind around deadlines and handy with that CTA to apply or enroll.

Name	High App Likelihood
Source	Subquery Filter
Type	Dependent subquery
Aggregate	Comparison
Field 1	Likelihood to Apply
Operator	>=
Field 2	80
Exports	Export
	Likelihood to Apply
	80

Criteria for a certain cutoff to receive MarComms can be programmed into the Deliver or the Rules to place them into Populations. The pictured example uses the Likelihood to Apply percent probability in a comparison Filer against a Literal value.

One possible shortcoming of this approach is the time in the cycle. If you want to send a drip campaign or even one-off emails to students likely to apply or enroll, but your records have not had enough time to get to 70, 80, 90 percent based on their behaviors, then your email will not be sent until far later in the cycle.

In these earlier stages (or if you want to communicate to the top 10th percentile of your records as opposed to a specific percent likely to enroll in general), a Translation Code may be the right solution. This example is built to solve a similar issue identifying "highly engaged" students throughout the cycle.

Downloading live data into Excel and using the Translation Code Update Excel Tab, automatically identifies the top X of students based on the current pool's likelihood values. This can also help staff not interested in the nuance of taking different actions on someone who is 89% likely to apply and someone 90% likely to apply so they can simply view a 1-5 value or text like "High", "Medium", and "Low" likely to apply.

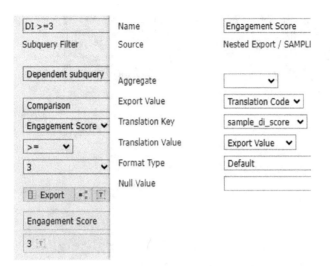

This screenshot uses the Translation Code in the Comparison Filter.

This example shows the actual Translation Code values and notes to describe each Export Value.

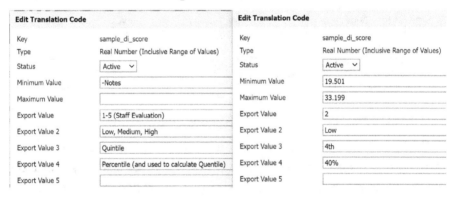

Lastly, this Excel document examines the data pulled from Slate to create the "bands" of likelihood to apply based on what values contain the top 20% of students, etc.

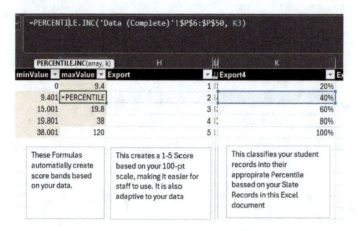

This allows you to continue to engage your highest likelihood to enroll regardless of the data or arbitrary cutoff.

Augment Content

Hi {{Person-First}},

Thank for for connecting with us {{Last-email-proxy}}! We hope you decide to apply by our deadline on {{'app_external_rd' | snippet: "deadlines"}}. if

{{Engagement-x-Application-Likelihood | snippet: "engagement_x_application_likelihood"}}
/if

Have a great holiday season!

While you can create standalone outreach specific for highly engaged or likely to behave students. You can also augment the content of a Deliver, Portal, or other outreach based on these values. The pictured example uses both Conditional Logic and Content Blocks driven by Scores and Modeling.

Conditional Logic is showing the content block for only a subset of the recipients (in this case, students with some combination of high or low Engagement Score and likelihood to apply, hiding it from the middle ground of students not needing the additional text.

A subquery export in the Recipient List builds the "Engagement-x-Application-Likelihood" value to pull the appropriate Content Block with a Concatenate and two formulas.

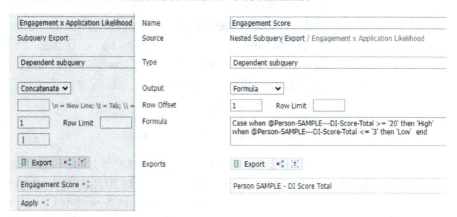

Each Content Block displays information or a Call To Action appropriate for the persona.

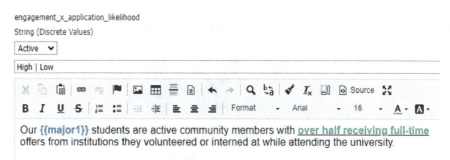

When the student has:

- High Engagement and High Likelihood –
    - Content about research with faculty. More just an opportunity to apply since the application deadline is coming up.

- High Engagement and Low Likelihood –
    - Talking about the experience and success of students in their Major. Help the student who loves our campus with practical outcomes that

may help motivate them (or their parents) to apply.

- Low Engagement and High Likelihood

  - Advertise in-person events. The student looks like someone who wants to attend, but they just haven't engaged with us. Better understanding may be what pushes them that last mile to apply.

- Low Engagement and Low Likelihood

  - Advertise virtual events and portal experiences. These students probably won't take a big Call To Action, but a virtual nudge is more realistic for them to take and could snowball their interest and likelihood to apply

Crafting Personas And Strategies

Simply combining likelihood to apply Model and Engagement Score is a... blunt way to augment MarComms, but it works as an example for this book.

Students who are already engaged or highly likely to enroll are also more likely to take a CTA or read a more in-depth email.

Hi Maya,

Thank for for connecting with us last week! We hope you decide to apply by our deadline on January 1st.

Tour (No), Virtual (No), Interview (No)
With temperatures that average 72 degrees, now is the best time to come for a Campus Tour at The University! Or if you can't make it to our neck of the woods, we run live Virtual Tours and even have an interactive virtual experience. You can always schedule time to interview with one of our Admission Counselors in person or virtually.
000

This is a similar email but is going just to your highly engaged or likely to apply, so you embed a dynamic CTA with Content Blocks. Highlighting the text with the corresponding data driving it as an example. Also showing the Export's value that is pulling the Content Block.

The export Concatenates three values. Each value is an Existence Export that checks if the students attended a type of event.

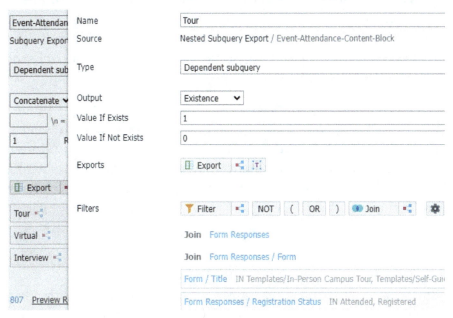

This export pulls Content Block(s) with the tailored CTA. Because you know they attended a specific type of event, you can reference and acknowledge that while highlighting how this new event recommendation compliments their previous engagements or expands on it somehow.

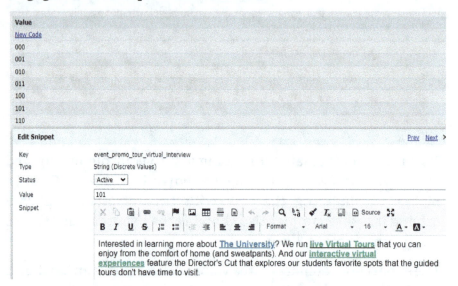

This is not to say engaged students should be sent long emails or multiple/complicated CTA's. Having seen several portals, pages, emails, and other MarComms that higher education puts out there (and reflecting upon my own), they're already entirely too long.

But as an industry, we do need to be better at meeting students where they are and curating their experience based on what is the best content for them to see *cough* Adaptive Enrollment Management *cough*. And these Scores are important factors that can help you tailor the messaging for where your students are in their journey.

Hi {{Person-First}},

Thank for for connecting with us {{Last-email-proxy}}!

You're also crafting this email with a reference to the last time the student reached out to the institution. Again, this helps meet the student where they're at in the journey through personalization and data utilization.

To get this effect, you calculate the last time the student emailed you. If your institution may have emails for other parties (school/CBO/Independent counselors, materials and other vendors, recommenders, parents, etc.) attached to the student's records, you will need to specify that the most recent email be limited to emails sent by the student's email.

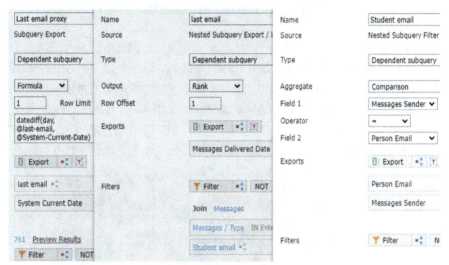

If students frequently change emails, using multiple comparisons or a coalesced series of personal emails compared to the Sender email may increase the accuracy of the last email sent by the student.

You will need to sort the messages by Date Sent to pull the most recent and use a translation code to make it conversational. You don't want to acknowledge they sent you an email 6 days ago. But simply say last week or month. Alternatively, you could reference an event that you met them at like a college fair, high school visit, or interview. The goal here is to connect with the student on a personal level - something other institutions likely aren't doing with automated emails that will read like a generic copy paste.

Connecting with students on a personal level becomes more

impactful the more information you have on their interests and what is motivating them.

If your institution does not currently ask students about why they're interested in going to college or what resources they value at your institution or what their evaluation/motivation around factors for enrolling at their institution, then you are missing out on incredibly informative data.

This can be done at the inquiry stage or at the very least in an Applicant/Admitted Student Survey. Moving beyond being explicitly told, tracking Ping data or conversation topics in Slate or using more ecospherical data with trends in ASC or 3rd party data of their neighborhoods can also help build this information and personas.

I'm a staunch proponent of as simple and streamlined of an RFI or event signup Form as possible. Name, birthdate, and email for the CRM and potential institutional needs like student type, entry term, school, and major. Maybe another question or two depending on what your institution absolutely needs to have a functioning relationship with this person. Spoiler alert though, you can just remove those 8 other questions you or someone in your office is clinging to desperately.

Beyond that, your confirmation page should redirect the student to a longer form, creating essentially a 2-page inquiry form. Even if you don't make all of your questions required, a 25-question RFI as the student's first or just early point of contact will be a stop-out for a lot of students.

```
<script>FW.Navigate('https://connect          /register/TellUsMore/?person=
{{Prospect-ID}}');</script>

     <script type="text/javascript">var delay = 10000; setTimeout(function(){
window.location = 'https://connect.          /register/TellUsMore/?person=
{{Prospect-ID}}'; }, delay);</script>
```

The second page is seamless enough that students who are interested and want to give you information will continue answering questions while the first page still completes those softer leads. This pictured example shows what you need to add to your HTML of the confirmation page. Important is adding and passing the student's Prospect ID or Person GUID to prefill the questions they just answered. This first option redirects the student immediately while the second allows the student to see the confirmation for a determined amount of time before being redirected.

An RFI example of collecting this additional information is in the following screenshot. In this form, it is asking the student what kinds of resources they are interested in - Academic, Cost, Campus, etc. as a multi-select question. For whichever resource these students click on, conditional logic displays follow-up questions for them to pick the highest priority sub-resource from those umbrella categories.

Proactively gathering similar information through mid-cycle surveys and questionnaires also gives you ample opportunities

to understand your students better.

Pitzer Resources ───────────

What kind of resources are you most interested about?
- ☑ Academic
- ☑ Activities
- ☑ Career
- ☑ Connections
- ☑ Cost
- ☑ Experience
- ☑ Campus
- ☑ I don't know yet

What Academic resource are you most interested in?
- ○ Facilities
- ○ Faculty
- ○ Reputation
- ○ Research
- ○ Support

What Activities resource are you most interested in?
- ○ Athletics
- ○ Clubs/Groups/Organizations
- ○ Community Service
- ○ Off-Campus Activities
- ○ Student Governance
- ○ Study Abroad

What Career resource are you most interested in?
- ○ Career Services Office
- ○ Exploring different Career Paths
- ○ Fellowhips
- ○ Internships
- ○ On-Campus Employment
- ○ Skills/Experiences

What Connections resource are you most interested in?
- ○ Alumni/parent/family
- ○ Community
- ○ Employers/organizations
- ○ Faculty Connections

What Cost resource are you most interested in?
- ○ Cost after grants and Scholarships
- ○ Financial Aid

What Experience resource are you most interested in?
- ○ First Generation
- ○ First Year Experience
- ○ Health
- ○ Interactions with People of Different Backgrounds
- ○ Sense of Community
- ○ Social Life
- ○ Traditions

What Campus resource are you most interested in?
- ○ Location
- ○ On-Campus Housing
- ○ Sustainability

What resource are you most interested in?
[_____ ▾]

Artisanal Curation

Automated comms and Portals featuring the information the student is interested in created a deeply connected student experience. Facilitating conversations around these topics with staff and faculty can unleash a hugely impactful enrollment strategy. Similarly, having current athletes reach out to students who are specifically interested in athletics or students currently participating in an internship or study abroad with prospects interested in those college experiences gives the prospective student a glimpse of what their experience will be like. It also shows them that you care about them to take this data and expand it into their engagements. Pairing this with recent alumni who are working in the industry or attending grad school with prospects who share those goals can have a profound impact on their enrollment decision.

You are beginning to curate a deeply personal relationship between the students, staff, faculty, and alumni with your prospective students in a way that randomly matching them would not have been able to do. But as your constituents are able to build those relationships and make an impact, not only will they be more likely to continue to participate, but they'll get others on board to join them. You are cutting down the barriers between your prospective students and your institution.

You demonstrate to your constituents that you value them, and you are not only curating the prospective student experience, but maximizing the impact the constituent has with a select student who is very specifically engaged and interested in their experience with teaching in a classrooms or studying abroad which you know that they did and would love to highlight.

These current constituents become mentors whether that's in the short-term or long-term to these prospective students. The bond that they start forming can be transformational both in the recruitment process but also as they become a student and continue to grow while on campus. This helps establish buy-in from your campus constituents but also establishes how sophisticated the institution is and how developed their network is that they are able to provide these kinds of interactions and relationships with prospective students. Being a mentor also carries its own benefits in boosting confidence, entrenching advice, and growing as a student.

As much effort, time and money as institutions spend in buying names, putting out ads, and curating social media, email, and text messaging; word of mouth is still an outstanding way to build brand and perceptions around your institution. Being able to curate such an exceptional experience for your students with limited resources and effort not only helps build your incoming class but establishes your institution as a true leader in the minds of students and those in their orbit.

Let's continue to take a step outside of just interests. There are a lot of reasons why students want to go to college or attend your institution specifically. A lot of this can be determined through questionnaires where students are explicitly telling you what they are interested in. BEACON data mining though allows you to go further with both Behavioral and Ecospherical indicators. Ping data or similar web tracking of students provide behavioral insight of your students and their interests (or concerns).

A student is not going to meander on various pages of your website for hours at a time, ingesting every morsel of information about your institution. Whether they came to your site organically or followed a link form your MarComms or some 3rd party, students want to know about the topics that are important to them. If the only link you send to your prospective students is a Sign Up of Events CTA, then perhaps Ping data may not be as relevant to you, but there should still be engagement on your website.

If your counselor has 2 students likely to enroll that they want to reach out to, then these virtual behaviors can help guide the interactions. If one student spent 10 minutes on a page about student/faculty research, 20 minutes on the biographies for an environmental studies faculty, and 10 minutes about careers in conservation, then you already have a grasp of what they want to do on campus, what they want to major in, and what they want to do after graduation. The institution already aligns with what they want. The engagement should focus on the fit and expanding upon it. It could also include faculty and students who have relevant experience in those things.

Alternatively, the other student spent 40 minutes on the Form I-20 page, 30 minutes on the financial aid page, and 20 minutes on the Net Tuition Calculator. There are more functional, operational, financial concerns around the college process that may prevent them from applying or enrolling that the counselor should focus on.

Similar student understanding can come from an even deeper level of inferred student data. Some vendors provide geographical trend data. Slate also comes preloaded with ACS (American Community Survey) data. Additional data from other sources like the Census Bureau could also be added to Slate to provide additional insights.

While frequently used with tools like Voyager, understanding the geographic trends allows you to understand and engage with students and parents in a way that likely speaks to their experience. Or at least the experience of those in their orbit - friends, family, neighbors, and colleagues. This also helps you build that student experience.

ACS data live in the World - US Zip Data by Data Points table.

While this can be done from the student's primary or mailing address, I am showing an example tied to the student's school address to demonstrate the "proper" way to pull school address.

Base — Configurable Joins - Person
Execution Mode — Retrieve all records each time query is run

Preview
Display !
Copy

Exports

Address 1 US 5-digit ZIP Code
World - US Zip Data by Data Point: % At least Grad/Prof education Value
World - US Zip Data by Data Point: % 200k+ Value
World - US Zip Data by Data Point: Median Household Value
World - US Zip Data by Data Point: % with broadband internet subscription Value

Filters   Check Logic   Query Profiler   Matching Rows: 1,798

Zip Code •⁝ Exists

Sorts

Joins

School 1   Rank = 1
School 1 / Organizations
Organizations / Address 1   Rank = 1
Address 1 / World - US Zip Data by Data Point: % At least Grad/Prof education   Data Point = Education - % At Least Graduate/Professional education
Address 1 / World - US Zip Data by Data Point: % 200k+   Data Point = Income - % $200k+
Address 1 / World - US Zip Data by Data Point: Median Household   Data Point = Income - Median Household
Address 1 / World - US Zip Data by Data Point: % with broadband internet subscription   Data Point = Technology - % With a broadband Internet subsc...

Joining from Person to School, School to Organization (the Slate table that houses your schools and associated validated data), Organization to Address. Each ACS datapoint requires a separate join to the World - US Zip Data by Data Points table and specifying which datapoint you want to pull into the Query.

209

Pro Tip: Renamed your joins to reflect the data you're pulling.

You can then export the "Value" of that join to understand the trends associated with that ZIP Code. This also unlocks communication strategies around likely relevant datapoints to the student. Students living with a high percentage of graduate/professional and bachelor degrees may be on a trajectory to go to grad school. And may have more support and expectation to attend college. While lower median income and percentage of owning a computer may benefit from greater assistance around the college application and journey.

Address 1 US 5-digit ZIP Code ▼ Value	World - US Zip Data by Data Point: % At least Grad/Prof education Value ↓T	World - US Zip Data by Data Point: % 200k+ Value ↓T	World - US Zip Data by Data Point: Median Household Value ↓T	World - US Zip Data by Data Point: % with broadband internet subscription Value ▼
60603	52.7	64.8 $	124,888	93.8
10022	47.3	60.6 $	161,236	93.4
75205	41.5	62.1 $	180,698	96.3
55105	38.7	41.8 $	112,162	95.4

Inferences made from this data can be used as standalone indicators to help guide conversations and automated communications. They can also be used to craft personas and populations to create communication and programming strategies around packages of interests.

Conclusion

When you - and your CRM - has a deep understanding of your students, your ability to communicate with them and build an enriching student journey that speaks directly to their experience builds the foundation of a mutual relationship. Each year, as you build more functionality and features, the relationships you build with prospective students and campus constituents gets richer and more fulfilling as you can curate both sides of the experience.

CHAPTER 16: GPS - RESOURCE ALLOCATION

GPS Resource Allocation - **G**uided **P**rioritization **S**trategy. Using Scoring and Predictive Modeling to prioritize high-cost and high-touch resources like staff/faculty/student phone calls, tailored print mailings, and person-centered interventions for students with a higher likelihood to apply or enroll to make a larger impact and ROI on your efforts.

Even as the Search Cliff and Demographic Cliff stack upon each other, choking funnels across higher education. Those funnels are still massive at nearly every stage, especially as institutions navigate tighter budgets and dwindling resources. Your counselors simply don't have the time to form deep, meaningful bonds with each of their students. And even if you wanted to send tailored view books curated to the student's interests, the cost to send thousands each year would be staggering. Not to mention attending every single college fair and high school visit across the country.

As beneficial as doing those things might be to the students on their college-going journey, the reality of higher education means that focusing efforts and resources allows your institution to provide these resources strategically and empowers you to make the impact where it will be felt most.

But how do you know who, what, and where to prioritize these limited resources? Well, believe it or not, you're already looking at it.

Engagement Scoring and Predictive Modeling paired together or taken separately will be the GPS on your path to prioritization - a Guided Prioritization Strategy. What can I say, I was molded by the world of acronyms around me.

This GPS system can be built into your processes in several ways with a variety of technical and strategic learning curves. Even though more of the student experience can be automated and optimized, the high-touch and high-cost elements are still essential to the recruitment and retention of students.

Guiding Work

Starting on the easier side of the prioritization charcuterie board, there's the rank-ordering of students by the likelihood of the student to apply/enroll (and/or high Engagement Score as a proxy or complimentary piece of information.

In the screenshot, a Slate report with two tables lists students for specific initiatives. The first table lists students using a filter of a 5 out of 5 Engagement Score (ran through your translation code to identify the highest percentile band of engaged students). These students will receive one of your high-cost/high-touch recruitment strategies like the admission counselor calling the student personally. This much smaller group of students allows the counselor to have more time dedicated to building that relationship with that high-impact population that will not only benefit from one-on-one counselor time but will also be more likely to enroll having received this intervention or programming.

Calls (Engagement Score 5/5)

First	Last	Email	DI Score Total	Staff Assigned
Bruce	Test	test8@gmail.com	70	David Dysart
Kitty	Test	test13@gmail.com	75	David Dysart
Kurt	Test	test7@gmail.com	80	David Dysart

This next table is limited to your 4 out of 5 Engagement Score students, and again, this could be an Engagement Score or a particular percentile band of your Score/Model. But what you're doing here is actually prioritizing another high-cost intervention. This one might not be as effective or might have a broader population that we want to use it on than the individualized calls reserved for 5 out of 5 students. Or the institutional action has been shown to be more effective for this particular group. So for this group of still very engaged but not quite as likely to apply students, you're going to send a highly personalized postcard or view book to them that help them understand the institution better and their place in it.

This can be done with a handwritten campaign or something like Slate Print that is utilizing Slate data and Content Blocks to deliver a personalized and curated experience but in an automatic fashion. Because this is a print project, it is going to have a substantially higher cost associated with it than a simple email campaign that is going to the broader funnel.

Post Cards (4/5)

First	Last	Email	DI Score Total	Staff Assigned
Alana	Steele	alana.steele@test.com	57.3	David Dysart
Serena	Sheppard	serena.sheppard@test.com	57.3	David Dysart
Addison	Bailey	addison.bailey@test.com	56.7	David Dysart
Audrey	Meyn	audrey.meyn@test.com	56.7	David Dysart

As many institutions are unable to afford such broad, scattershot recruitment strategies to the entire population (or even if they could, would benefit from more strategic resource allocation than thousands of unread postcards and viewbooks), GPS gives the institution the opportunity to still engage with the student on this personalized level at a reduced cost and with higher return on investment since we are targeting students who are more likely to have their needle moved by these projects.

These tables use the Engagement Score/predictive model values to filter and limit the number of students displayed. In this case, paired with a translation code transforming the raw Score or percentage into simpler, meaningful, and practical Score bands.

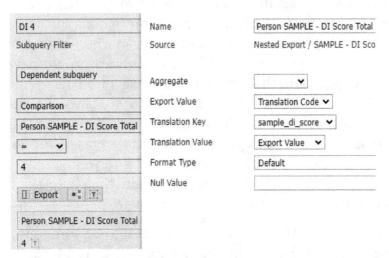

This process helps with intra-cycle changes as your institution and students progress through recruitment. With your goal to engage with your high likelihood to apply students, you may be planning to work with 70, 80, 90% likely to apply, but early in the cycle, the highest values you may have is in the 20s because students haven't engaged with your institution in as many meaningful ways. You can't wait until you have a higher percent likelihood to apply just to start working with these students.

This Translation Code is built on top of your current Slate pool. Who is in the top 20th percentile? The next band? Or who are the 20 most engaged students per admission counselor? A 1-5 or a specific task name or description are added to these students through the Translation Code.

Edit Translation Code

Key	sample_di_score
Type	Real Number (Inclusive Range of Values)
Status	Active
Minimum Value	-Notes
Maximum Value	
Export Value	1-5 (Staff Evaluation)
Export Value 2	Low, Medium, High
Export Value 3	Quintile
Export Value 4	Percentile (and used to calculate Quentile)
Export Value 5	

Edit Translation Code

Key	sample_di_score
Type	Real Number (Inclusive Range of Values)
Status	Active
Minimum Value	19.501
Maximum Value	33.199
Export Value	2
Export Value 2	Low
Export Value 3	4th
Export Value 4	40%
Export Value 5	

With your current pools added to Excel, the Upload Dataset formatted for Translation Codes uses formulas to analyze your current data to assign these values. These cutoffs can change to be a different method or whatever specification will fit your bandwidth. This allows you to almost cohort your work allowing students to enter and leave what is essentially a population.

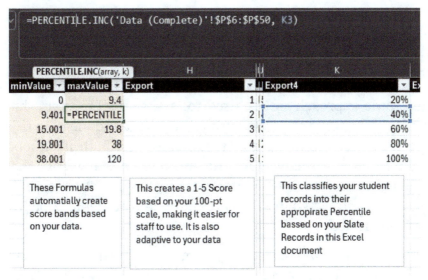

```
=PERCENTILE.INC('Data (Complete)'!$P$6:$P$50, K3)
```

minValue	maxValue	Export		Export4		Ex
0	9.4		1			20%
9.401	=PERCENTILE		2			40%
15.001	19.8		3			60%
19.801	38		4			80%
38.001	120		5			100%

These Formulas automatially create score bands based on your data.

This creates a 1-5 Score based on your 100-pt scale, making it easier for staff to use. It is also adaptive to your data

This classifies your student records into their appropirate Percentile bassed on your Slate Records in this Excel document

Slate Populations may get you to this same spot internally built with Rules, but most ways to specify the bands will be more difficult in Slate, and this Excel process wouldn't take more than half an hour (assuming you spent half that time also putting out another fire or taking a call from a concerned parent). This adaptive framework allows you to stay within bandwidth, budget, and benefit.

Likelihood to Enroll >= 80%

Metric	Total	Low GPA	STEM Programs	Fin Aid
Total	111	37	42	104
Location / School by Rank Overall Code				
CA-23 Covina & West Covina	56	18	20	53
High School of Academics	28	9	9	28
University of Beyond Acad...	28	9	11	25
CA-27 Riverside, San Bernard...	55	19	22	51
Beyond College Academics	27	10	10	26
United Academics of Beyo...	28	9	12	25
STEM				
Biological Sciences	4	1	4	4
Biology	4	1	4	4
Computer Science	4	1		4
Data Science	4	2	4	3
Engineering	7	3	7	6
Information and Computer Sci...	7	3	7	7
Information Sciences	7	2	7	7
Mathematics	6	3	6	6
Mechanical Engineering	3	2	3	1
Nursing	4			4

Low GPA

First	Last	Email	School by Rank Overall GPA	DI Score Total	Staff Assigned
Blake	Nelson	blake.nelson@test.com	2.7	20.0	David Dysart
Alvin	Austin	alvin.austin@test.com	2.7	0.0	David Dysart
Eleanor	Dilts	eleanor.dilts@test.com	2.7	0.0	David Dysart
Preston	Esquivel	preston.esquivel@test.com	2.7	5.8	David Dysart

This same approach can be used to create small clusters that faculty can engage and help with recruitment and yield. In this screenshot, you're looking at students with a high likelihood to enroll. You're seeing your incoming class that meets that criteria, but also three populations - lower GPA/Academic Readiness, interested in STEM programs, and students applying for financial aid.

Within these four columns, you're then breaking this out into geography/corresponding school, the individual STEM programs, and a listing of your students with lower academic readiness. The first and last we will tackle in our SCOUT and THRIVE chapters.

So let's look at your Programs. If your admission counselors did not have the bandwidth to reach out to all of your prospective students individually, your faculty certainly don't have the bandwidth (or want) to do that for those students or even just your incoming class.

Prioritizing this list gives these constituents a much more manageable group of students to interact with who are already likely to enroll but may need an additional nudge. And being connected with current faculty, students, or even alumni in the program can be a huge... NUDGE.

This becomes an even more powerful GPS when paired with additional data gathered in the BEACON data collection and mining. If your population of stem students are indicating that they are particularly interested in academics such as the facilities, faculty, research etc., then the list of students for faculty to interact with can be limited even more. The high likelihood to enroll STEM students more interested in on-campus housing, internships, etc. could be better served hearing from other institutional constituents, allowing faculty to engage with the students they'd make the biggest impact with.

Changes In Behavior

Having the GPS in place to help segment your pool allows you to be more strategic and make more meaningful impacts on the students and incoming class. While prioritizing students with a high level of engagement or likelihood to perform an outcome like applying or enrolling, other key behavioral insights allow you to prioritize your work.

The Feature Engineering chapter covered several ways to cut and combine data to float unique situations to the top of your pool. Recent engagement is a good variable to add to a Scoring rubric - whether that's the number of emails sent by the student or website Ping traffic in the last thirty days or weighting more recent behavior heavier than older behaviors.

This example counts the number of emails sent by the student within the last 30 days. The second pop-up has several relevant filters for querying emails sent. The Method allows you to specify "Email" as opposed to other data on that table like SMS, Letters, Mail Merges, Voice, etc.

The Type also specifies you want External Messages coming into Slate as opposed to Deliver Mailings, Form Communications, and Ad Hoc Messages all sent from Slate.

Lastly, you will want to specify the email address sending the email is the student's email as emails merely attached to the record from parents, counselors, vendors providing material, etc. will also be included without this filter which are not going to be as predictive as actual messages from the student.

These students that are exhibiting high recent engagement should also be prioritized, even if they do not have a high Score or predicted Model value. They might be new to the pool, so they have not engaged enough to rise into the top prospect population. Or they have just recently started to seriously consider your institution. Either way, these hot prospects are great candidates to do those high-cost, high-touch outreach for as well. Even if you don't have a Score or Model at all yet, this is a much lower cost to just identify these candidates that are heating up.

A highly engaged or likely to apply student may have recently decided against your institution, but the above students are the ones with their interests peaked. It is important to examine decreases in engagement. If a student is disengaging with your institution, they may have committed to another school or simply be losing interest. In the latter case, having their counselor reach out to them or some other kind of targeted action may put your institution back to the top of their list.

In this example. The student sent at least five emails in the last 180 days. But they sent zero emails in the last 30 days. These criteria could also use other anchors like Engagement Score greater than thirty but zero engagements (emails, Ping, events) after Decision Received, Campus tour, Financial Aid Meeting, etc. This could be strongly indicative of a change in enrollment probability.

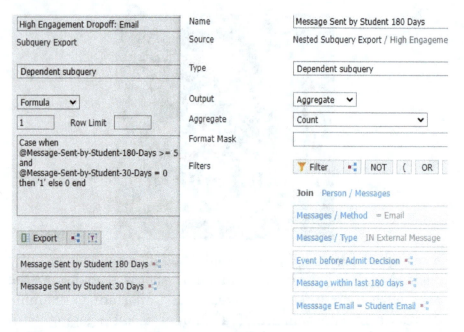

Several other variables we built in the Feature Engineering chapter would also be relevant indicators and milestones that the student should be prioritized. If you skipped that chapter, but plan to implement a GPS system, I would highly recommend at least skimming it and incorporating some ideas into your system.

While I showed some examples of reports that can be used to guide counselor actions through a GPS, creating a staff portal with the Reports and details embedded into them will create a much simpler and straightforward process. This continues to be true when the portal can be a hub where the staff have access to the broader roles, tasks, and responsibilities they have. Tools like Content Blocks allow these portals to be personalized to the staff so they only see what's relevant to them. It also allows you to float outstanding action items (e.g. a feedback form on your new Engagement Score rubric).

Paired with a dynamic main tab that uses the current date in context of the projects and tasks that they are most likely to be working on that day allows them to have a fast and frictionless work environment.

Title	Start Time	Registrants	Incl. guests	Staff	Launch Check-In
Campus Tour	09:00 AM	2	6		id=90736ce7-d8fd-45aa-884c-efeb7b863195
Information Session	10:00 AM	2	6		id=cfe34d13-1cdd-4311-b5a0-98edf9078e86
Campus Tour	11:00 AM	1	1		id=1cdbaabc-138d-4d1f-8908-01a4d1253feb
Campus Tour	01:00 PM	1	2		id=b2081580-446f-40a8-bc1c-78f30d79e534
Information Session	02:00 PM	2	4		id=4b64d226-6cf9-49cc-94b7-158e28ac7513
Campus Tour	03:00 PM	1	2		id=8916ab45-1603-4238-bd31-84f718c3e049

There's a lot of great work being done on both the institutional and vendor side building general staff portals as well as portals designed specifically to guide counselor outreach. I'd recommend viewing conference slides and webinars to take some design cues and inspiration. Both Carnegie and Waybetter both come to mind as examples of what can be done in this space, and they bring a great level of polish to their respective counselor portals.

Conclusion

Implementing a GPS using Engagement Scoring and Predictive Modeling empowers higher education institutions to allocate high-cost, high-touch resources more effectively. Examining how the behaviors of your students change also provides insights on who you need to engage with, especially around the moment that matter.

By focusing efforts on students with a higher likelihood to apply or enroll or other indicators, institutions can maximize impact and ROI amidst tightening budgets and resource constraints. This strategic approach not only enhances recruitment and retention but also ensures meaningful engagement with students, ultimately navigating the challenges posed by the evolving higher education landscape.

CHAPTER 17: SCOUT RECRUITMENT - PRACTICES

SCOUT Recruitment: **S**trategic **C**ommunity **O**utreach and **U**niversity **T**ravel. A recruitment strategy that focuses on identifying trends and forming strategies around recruitment efforts - including travel, building relationships, leveraging fit dynamics, and augmenting outreach to enhance engagement and boost enrollment outcomes.

Recruitment Travel

If you created three pie charts - staff hours used, dollars spent, and staff's evaluation of importance, how dominant are the slices for recruitment travel in each of those charts? Assuming your institution does recruitment travel, probably pretty large slices.

SCOUT Recruitment is not just about recruitment travel, but if your institution does do recruitment travel, applying SCOUT to your strategy will likely have its biggest impact on which schools and fairs you visit.

Now, how many more students are enrolling at your institution because of those visits? Are new names flowing into your CRM from them? Making connections with existing records? What are the application and enrollment behaviors of those two groups of students and how do they differ from the other groups in your prospect pool?

Let's peel back another layer. What's the impact of your recruitment travel at the schools you do travel for? Perhaps from School A, there's an influx of applications after a visit - both for attendees and the broader population. Or you get more applications than you'd expect based on their Engagement Score or Modeling value.

School B on the other hand continues being an underperforming school. Even with travel to the school, students apply at a lower rate than anticipated. Or perhaps School B does apply more frequently but only with a more experienced recruiter at the event. Or someone with a similar background or interest as the students.

How do application rates differ when skipping travel to that school for a year? At an over-performing school like School A, this can be a scary proposition. Does your institution have a strong enough bridge to skip travel there for a year? Or does the recruiter's presence there tie the relationship together?

What about School B? Why are you still traveling there? Because it's a third school close to two over-performing schools? Because 5 years ago, it was considered a feeder school? Because it was next to the recruiter's favorite BBQ restaurant and the three subsequent recruiters never questioned why it was on the itinerary?

With high cost recruitment like travel, things like tradition, inertia, and repetition are not only a waste of time and money, but they can actively hurt you from traveling to untapped schools and markets that need a nudge to become feeder schools.

Let's start with why do you visit a region or school for travel?

Perhaps the school or region is a feeder that applies, gets admitted, or enrolls at a high level. Why are they doing that? Is their college counselor an alum? Or do they have a really good relationship with the recruiter from your institution? So your institution and its resources come up in conversations around attending college.

Or maybe your institution is a great fit for the students who also attend that school. There's a strong conservational culture both at the school and your institution.

You're a STEM college, and that high school has a great program for students interested in physics or interest in the sciences. Or there's an amazing physics teacher that follows the research and publications of your faculty, so they connect their lessons to the groundbreaking work being done at your institution. Perhaps your institution has a great blog post or public-facing piece by a staff of faculty that the counselor sends students to who then engage with your institution.

There could also be an existing bridge between the schools. Their older friends and siblings attend your institution and sing your praises. Or alumnae come back and get great jobs or are making impacts in their community, so they have aspiration role models who have proven the value of attending your institution.

It could be a combination of those things, but as you start investigating the answer, some trends are likely to become clear. If it is a large number of current students who are unofficially proselytizing their program, experience, or success, this can allow you to use these students as more official or paid student ambassadors so you can continue to leverage this peer-to-peer strategy. Those current students can increase their outreach to that broader geography or similar communities where their work will speak to.

Similar students can also be hired to replicate the original work in their own communities and networks. Even if you haven't found out what exactly is the lightning in the bottle, adding current students into the marketing and communication process at any (but hopefully all) levels can improve the work and impact.

Prospective students want authentic content. They also want to hear from current students. But even beyond generating content, having current students embedded in the strategy and review of content empowers you to more faithfully adapt to your target audience.

Engagements

You also need to understand how different geographies,

populations, distances, schools, and groups engage and interact with you. This extends to things like campus visits at your institution. Students at your local high school probably attend at a higher rate than that average out-of-state school. It's faster, easier, and cheaper for local students to visit campus. What's the relationship between visiting campus and applying for a local student? How does that differ for an out of state student? International?

What motivates an out-of-state student to visit your campus? What levers can you pull or when is the best time for a campus visit Call To Action? You can pester every student in every email with a link to visit campus, but what better CTA could you have delivered that they would have taken and become more engaged with your institution?

And even from a more aggregate level, there are follow-up questions you need to ask though? What schools are visiting your campus? What trends, connections, and motivators are pushing students to take such a large engagement with your institution? Is there an influx of students from Wisconsin that visit your California campus in November? Targeted recruitment in winter time that features your weather allows you to segment your MarComms to speak to the student's situation at a time when they want a change.

There are so many reasons why your institution can resonate with students at a school. So many relationships that can be fostered. Many ways for interests to be cultivated. Understanding and leveraging existing success provides direction and goals to be used elsewhere, especially at similar schools.

Once you understand what behaviors have the biggest impacts on your outcomes, and what can be used to motivate those populations to take these behaviors, you can be more strategic with how you recruit and NUDGE specific groups of students.

Search

Student Search, lead names, purchased names. There are a lot of terms for it. And a lot of vendors where institutions can acquire names… for a price.

This book is no more about the Search Cliff than the Enrollment Cliff. But legal and privacy limitations are compounding the complication of fewer students taking the test in a test-optional and test-free environment (even if many schools are inching back to the warm embrace of testing). This stacks on top of another issue - fewer students to take the test and engage in other vendors that pass along names to institutions.

Even if those issues weren't bearing down on institutions, how data-driven is your institution's name-buying strategy. How current is it? How do the students convert and perform? How much is your institution paying per matriculated student?

While Engagement Scoring and Predictive Modeling may be less effective ways to measure the effectiveness of your strategy than examining the various conversion rates, understanding how they behave in the Engagements Scores and Subscores, especially in context of other groups as well as building Search-specific Models to examine the data and weights that lead them to apply and enroll can shed a very interesting light in what these groups look like.

The methods in this book, especially BEACON Data Mining and

SCOUT Recruitment provide very helpful lenses to be more strategic with how and which names you purchase.

There are a myriad of other issues with name acquisition - unreliable performance, population-specific trends of test taking and timeline availability, use of names sourced in this way, over-reliance on third-party sources, etc. etc. etc. This really isn't a book on that (as I keep whispering to myself).

The other element of this book that is critical as it relates to Search is optimization of your funnel. Search Names are a huge slice of the top of the funnel and a much smaller slice of the enrolling class.

If you need to enroll 10 more students, let's look at how we can accomplish this in a couple more ways

- Current
  - 100,000 Prospects
  - 5,000 Applications (5% Application Rate)
  - 2,500 Admits (50% Admit Rate)
  - 250 Students (10% Yield Rate)
- Bigger Funnel
  - 300 Student Goal
  - 3,000 Admits (500 more admits)
  - 6,000 Applications (1,000 more applicants)
  - 120,000 Prospects (20,000 more names purchased)
- Better Funnel
  - 300 Student Goal (20% Yield Rate)
  - 1,500 Admits (50% Admit Rate)

- 3,000 Applications (10% Application Rate)

- 30,000 Prospects (70,000 fewer names purchased)

Through buying names more in tune with your institution and leveraging Adaptive Enrollment Management, you met your goal, achieved better yield rates from your admits, and converted more of your purchased names. In fact, instead of buying 20,000 additional names, you reduced the number by 70,000 names.

Granted, these numbers were arbitrary, and not something that you will snap your fingers after reading this book to achieve by next cycle. But there are a lot of struggling and comfortable institutions that are in for hard times ahead.

As fewer students graduate from high school, more students choose alternatives to college, and the students who do pursue higher education apply to more colleges, commit at a larger number, and face more barriers to enrolling, succeeding, and graduating; institutions will find themselves having to do more with less. Maybe the above strategies are not even to get 50 additional students. In a couple years, you might need to do one of the above just to stay at current levels. Or maybe you needed to do them a couple years ago to keep from dropping.

So many people want a bigger funnel to solve their problems.

But their problem is inside the funnel. You may not think your institution can convert better, but after almost 70 years of runners trying to break the 4-minute mile, once people saw Bannister do it, multiple people IN A SINGLE RACE ran sub 4-minute miles a year later.

When we disregard the impossible or even learn what is possible - that a peer institution has a 40% applicant rate from search names or a 50% app rate from travel, we can start looking at how we can truly improve what's happening in our funnel.

Conclusion

The SCOUT Recruitment strategies focus your efforts through the lens of your current data, successes, and failures. Leveraging the relationships and populations that outperform expectations unlocks new paths and avenues for you to explore in your recruitment, engagement, and search efforts. And as you reallocate resources from underperforming to higher impact efforts, they will continue to compound and grow exponentially.

CHAPTER 18: SCOUT RECRUITMENT - SLATE

SCOUT Recruitment: **S**trategic **C**ommunity **O**utreach and **U**niversity **T**ravel. A recruitment strategy that focuses on identifying trends and forming strategies around recruitment efforts - including travel, building relationships, leveraging fit dynamics, and augmenting outreach to enhance engagement and boost enrollment outcomes.

Slate

Much of the previous chapter has been a string of questions. But so much of the connection and why behind recruitment travel is institution-specific. It will require close examination of your data and not only why students are attending recruitment travel or applying, but also why the institution is doing that travel.

Pushback that I received while working on integrating SCOUT was that travel to schools was not only to improve the connection and affinity to the institution but also to reach communities to improve college access and help bridge the students to college more broadly.

Even with that, you can still use the SCOUT methodology to guide both institutional success and student success. Incorporated ACS data and external sources from vendors and Census Bureau to Slate can help identify communities that outreach can be impactful, especially where it can be reached while still being able to increase the functional prospect pool for the institution.

In this Slate Report, you can start piecing together funnel performance for schools or other ways to slice your populations apart -

| Schools | | | | | | |
School	Records	Applicants	Matriculants	Ave: Eng. Score	Ave: Likelihood to Apply	Relative Outcomes
	110	19	1	32	35	Low Apps
	245	141	36	21	35	High Apps
	248	116	34	20	32	Expected
	243	70	23	70	32	High Eng.

- School 1:
    - **Data:** Students have high levels of engagement and reasonable application likelihood
    - **Outcome:** Students apply at a lower rate than projected (<10%) and matriculate at a lower rate than peers and broader pool
    - **Action:** Unless there's a compelling reason to continue recruitment travel or some way to dramatically improve the impact, the time and resources spent here could be used to drastically better ends elsewhere.

- School 2:

    - **Data:** Students have low-ish levels of engagement and reasonable application likelihood

    - **Outcome:** Students apply at a much higher rate than projected (>55%)

    - **Action:** There is some secret sauce here that needs to be understood and leveraged elsewhere to improve enrollment outcomes. It may also inform the Predictive Modeling

- School 3:

    - **Data:** Students have low levels of engagement and reasonable application likelihood

    - **Outcome:** Students still apply at a slightly elevated rate, but reasonably on track

    - **Action:** Experiment with ways to increase engagement. Students already apply at higher rates even with exceptionally low engagement. Further building the relationship and increasing engagement may create a rockstar feeder school

- School 4:

    - **Data:** Students have very high levels of engagement and reasonable application likelihood

    - **Outcome:** Students have a very elevated level of engagement than typically seen with their likelihood to apply. They also apply at a lower rate than projected.

    - **Action:** Students are extremely engaged but

there's a barrier to applying. Perhaps the cost to attend, low pathways or outcomes associated with their interests, or some kind of bad word of mouth. Or maybe their school's name is misspelled in your application... Investigate! You're close to success with this school.

Not only does this process allow you to prioritize recruitment travel, it sheds light on the relationships you have with your schools. Further investigation allows you to leverage the wins elsewhere or break down barriers to empower students who want to win to cross the finish line.

Peeling this report apart in an external software like Excel or Tableau allows you to look at this more granularly and with more focus, including looking at year-over-year trends.

I would recommend not only using recruitment travel event attendance but coding schools and areas where recruitment travel is happening (which admittedly is more difficult at Fairs).

You are investigating the relationships and connection your institution has with institutions. That requires understanding the engagements but also classifying these groups. What is the culture? What do students want from college? What are their plans after college? We're getting further into BEACON data mining, but when you understand the student trends, you can tailor not only your emails but also how you approach broader recruitment like travel, building relationships, and CTAs.

Let's revisit the ACS data discussed in the GPS chapter. As opposed to looking at the ACS data as it relates to an individual student's possible experience, you can look at the nature of these geographies to guide recruitment travel and student search purchases.

In this report, you have ZIP codes listed. Again, we're using this as an example. This could be any kind of trait, persona, or group that you're examining as it relates to your recruitment.

You are pulling the relevant characteristics associated with the ZIP code but also institutional metrics like funnel status, Yield Rate. I would recommend using a Dataset to build this table with your group like ZIP Code. That also lets you set characteristics and classifications for those values to focus for this reporting and adds insights when you need additional information on the geographies.

Addresses

ZIP Code	% 15 to 19 Years Old	# Enrolled in High School	% Industry - Information	# of Records	# of Apps	# of Enrolling	Yield Rate	Ave Engagement Score	Ave Likelihood to Apply
10022	2.2	514	6.1						
75205	12.6	1601	3.6						
92407	8	4326	0.8						

Student characteristics need to be pulled through Independent Subqueries. Filtering with a Comparison lets you compare the student's ZIP code with the value in the Row to get values associated with the proper row.

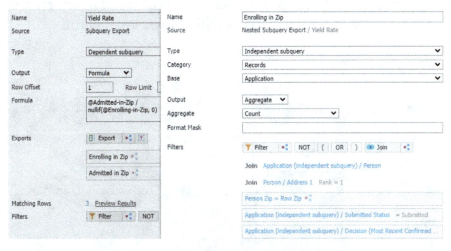

As the group's demographics and student behaviors align with institutional needs, recruitment travel can be devised to make the greatest impact while reducing travel that does not further student and institutional success.

This also opens the door for spreading to untapped markets. You can look at funnel performance against engagement Scores and projected application and enrollment outcomes.

Once you identify the overperforming locations, you can examine what resonates about your institution to those students to leverage it in other locations.

This SCOUT dissection of groups opens up new strategy paths for your institution to pursue. As data becomes a larger driver of that strategy, increased success will follow close behind.

Voyager

For the visually inclined, you can also look at the data through the Voyager tool. A good first step is just finding where your pools of students are and how dense they are. Filters allow you to also identify highly engaged or high likelihood to apply/enroll for even more targeted and prioritized recruitment.

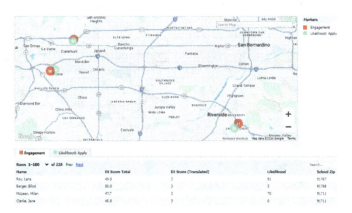

But one of the beautiful things about Voyager is the ability to easily overlay with ACS data. In this example, you're able to see what percent have at least a Bachelor's degree.

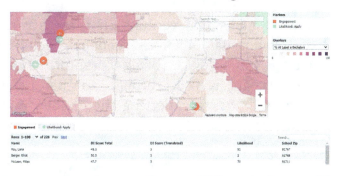

Voyager can also be used on different bases like your Organizations. This allows you to see your feeder schools. The filter pictured here gives you a cutoff to quantify what a "feeder" school is for you.

Again, because this is an Independent Subquery, you will need to Aggregate the Count by comparing the student's School CEEB Code to the Organization's (the current Query Base) Key.

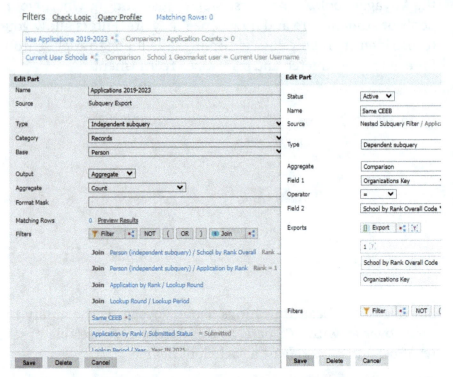

You'll also want additional context on these organizations. If you have vendor data like the school or neighborhood's cluster/challenge value, you can bring that information in from your broader student records through another Independent Subquery. Pictured, you're exporting the Challenge Indicator from your student records.

Edit Part

Status	Active ▾
Name	Projected School Challenge
Source	Subquery Export
Type	Independent subquery ▾
Category	Records ▾
Base	Person ▾
Output	Concatenate ▾
Row Separator	\n = New Line; \t = Tab; \\ = Escaped Backslash
Row Offset	1 Row Limit 1
Export Separator	
Exports	🗍 Export ⁝⁝ 🔢
	Person (independent subquery) High School - Overall Challenge Indicat...

Some additional work is needed for the filter of the Export. You again need to match the student's school CEEB to the Organization Key. This data at the time of writing is only provided to applicants that were manually uploaded and downloaded from the vendor, so an additional Existence export is needed to ensure the first record that matches the school actually has a value to bring into the Query. Bring existing data from another student in that Zip Code who does have a value, unlocking this data for other students, organizations, and the actual geographies.

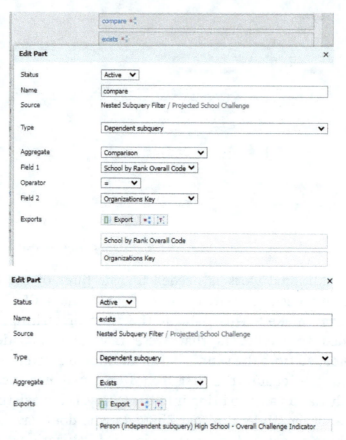

Similarly, Aggregates can be brought into the Query to identify things like the number of applications, average Engagement Score, yield rate, etc.

Voyager is also a good way to evaluate events like school visits and college fairs. Starting at a Form Base gives you more direct access to the event. One way to improve the Voyager is to scope the results to the user's assigned territory. This can be tricky if staff change recruitment territories, but using Translation Codes to do staff assigned can also be used in the filters to match the logged in User to the Coalesce of the Form address or the associated school's address. This Geomarket uses a Translation Code to return the User associated with it, even if that staff is not the associated User.

If you have not implemented Translation Code Staff Assignment, I HIGHLY recommend it. It's immensely valuable, flexible, and powerful. One note would be that the functionality does not replicate to writing a value into a Prompt-driven field as I learned 3/4 into a project I had begun based solely on the principle that I could stitch it together with the same process. There is a SQL workaround, but not necessarily advisable as Slate continues to move away from Custom SQL solutions.

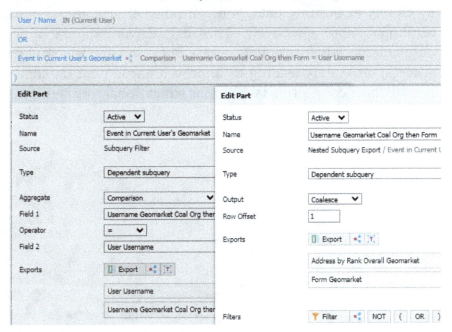

Analyzing existing data and trends empowers you to be more proactive with your recruitment strategy, which can be especially impactful when allocating the time, money, and resources required for recruitment travel.

Even if your institution is not able to travel to new/different locations, targeting virtual experiences, especially live ones, help build relationships with the students there and allows you to build a bridge between the schools.

And continuing to nurture the relationship your institution

has with official and unofficial ambassadors and counselors can continue to strengthen new and existing bridges alike.

Conclusion

Leveraging SCOUT Recruitment through tools like Slate Report and Voyager empowers you to optimize recruitment strategies and deepen relationships with prospective students and schools. By closely examining data, you can tailor efforts and allocate resources more effectively. This data-driven approach not only enhances institutional success but also supports student success, ultimately leading to improved enrollment outcomes and stronger connections within the educational community.

CHAPTER 19: THRIVE PROGRAMMING

THRIVE: **T**argeted **H**uman-centered **R**esources and **I**ntervention for **V**ital **E**mpowerment. A prescriptive Modeling strategy that empowers institutions to proactively deliver tailored programming that helps students succeed. By investing in recruitment and student success through customized support based on predictive analytics, THRIVE ensures students not only enroll but truly flourish at the university.

Given this book's focus on Admission work, we'll be applying THRIVE through a recruitment lens. Let's first revisit our GPS Report. You are examining your data for opportunities to curate programming that speaks to your prospective students.

As a refresher, you're examining three groups of students that may or may not be mutually exclusive. The important piece is that the programming designed for these three will be different.

Students may then opt into the one(s) that most speak to them.

Financial Aid

Likelihood to Enroll >= 80%

Metric	Total	Low GPA	STEM Programs	Fin Aid
Total	111	37	42	104
Location / School by Rank Overall Code				
CA-23 Covina & West Covina	56	18	20	53
	28	9	9	28
	28	9	11	25
CA-27 Riverside, San Bernardi...	55	19	22	51
	27	10	10	26
	28	9	12	25

The largest population of the three is that group that historically applies for financial aid. After further investigation you may discover that one of the clusters of schools has a higher average need of financial aid or if paired with additional data, that first group might have a higher challenge index or lower college attainment.

So while holding an event in a central location could be chosen to try to get students from both clusters, it may be more likely to get fewer students than hosting a Case Study or Application Workshop with a Financial Aid Counselor in attendance. This event could then be held closer to the institutions with higher need students.

Stem

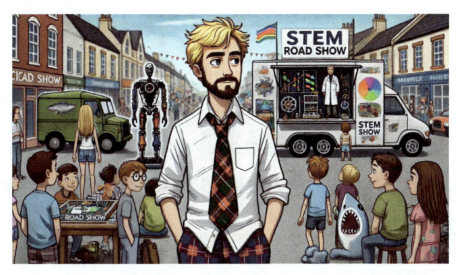

In a similar situation with a high level of interest in STEM, then including a professor or student in your recruitment can have a larger impact at those institutions. By sending one from a STEM major at your institution allows you to connect the genuine interests of the students while talking with someone who is in the classes that they will be taking.

These unique recruiters can also speak to the student experience and career outcomes in a way many admission counselors cannot know for what is likely a broad array of majors at the university.

And with a high concentration of prospective students who want to hear about the unique recruiter's perspective, this is a good way to get additional buy-in from these constituents to become more engaged and involved in recruitment.

That's not to say they will only discuss the classes/major. There will be many prospective students who are not interested in those particular classes, but these recruiters will bring a variety of insightful and interesting experiences. Deploying them where their interests will have the largest overlap with the prospective students just allows you to build on that synergy.

Academic Barrier

Likelihood to Enroll >= 80%

Metric	Total	Low GPA	STEM Programs	Fin Aid
Total	111	37	42	104
Location / School by Rank Overall Code				
CA-23 Covina & West Covina	56	18	20	53
	28	9	9	28
	28	9	11	25
CA-27 Riverside, San Bernardi...	55	19	22	51
	27	10	10	26
	28	9	12	25

STEM				
Biological Sciences	4	1	4	4
Biology	4	1	4	4
Computer Science	4	1		4
Data Science	4	2	4	3
Engineering	7	3	7	6
Information and Computer Sci...	7	3	7	7
Information Sciences	7	2	7	7
Mathematics	6	3	6	6
Mechanical Engineering	3	2	3	1
Nursing	4			4

Low GPA

First	Last	Email	School by Rank Overall GPA	DI Score Total	Staff Assigned
Blake	Nelson	blake.nelson@test.com	2.7	20.0	David Dysart
Alvin	Austin	alvin.austin@test.com	2.7	0.0	David Dysart
Eleanor	Dilts	eleanor.dilts@test.com	2.7	0.0	David Dysart
Preston	Esquivel	preston.esquivel@test.com	2.7	5.8	David Dysart

The report also lists students with academic barriers - "Low GPA" for this example. Additional details can be brought into the Report or personas. In this scenario, you are beginning to craft an Academic Preparedness Workshop during the new student onboarding to help students hit the ground running once classes start. This could also include connection with mentors, tutors, or other resources. It also allows students to form cohorts with each other and build that support system with students going through the same challenges. This last piece can also help students with imposter syndrome, especially on a campus where the broader population might not obviously reflect their background and/or struggles.

While you may not place students into the program,

communication or advertisement could be focused around the student who could benefit the most from.

This could also be any number of indicators that might flag potential barriers to success. From predicting lower chances of retention to having responsibilities outside of college that may pull them from their studies. The different barriers often have different remedies, but with an analysis of the data, you can begin allocating the resources in a data-driven way.

These individualized programming efforts not only allow you to connect and support your prospective students in a meaningful way, but it also demonstrates a culture of caring, success, and personalization that can increase their sense of belonging.

And as with recruitment, perhaps 75% of incoming students could benefit at least mildly from this additional programming. Even if we can look past the cost of this kind of heavily personalized programming and preparation, delivering the program to a substantially smaller percent of your incoming class will have a more profound impact to those attending - likely including most of the students who would have dropped out, been put on academic probation, or had a negative experience transitioning to college. The needle moves much further for this smaller cohort than increasing first-year GPA .02 for that broader 75% of the incoming class.

Evaluating Success

Let's look at the programming effectiveness in increasing yield. You can use Predictive Modeling to measure the effectiveness as an experiment/pilot. You can do this in a couple ways. Assuming your Predictive Modeling is reliable, you can evaluate how successful a new program is by evaluating the enrollment behavior compared to the predicted enrollment behavior.

Alternatively, you can use the predictive model to identify

a group of students who are suitable comparisons for the treatment and control groups. This will be easier than building a propensity score. And the group probably is not appropriate or large enough for a merely randomized study.

N	O	P	Q
Post-Experiment: In-State			
Groups	**Admits**	**Yield**	**Enrolled**
In-State	65	69%	45
- Experiment Group	20	80%	16
- Received Phone Call	10	90%	9
- No Call (Control)	10	70%	7
- Other Students	45	64%	29

This example takes your 65 In-State admits. Twenty were identified with similar likelihoods to enroll. Ten were randomly chosen to receive the programming while the other ten matched admits received no additional outreach.

The admits receiving the programming had a yield rate of 90% while the matched admits only yielded at 70%. Both groups were already high-likelihood to attend, making this smaller group of students both high-impact and a manageable number to receive these resource-intensive initiatives.

With a new initiative shown to be effective for this group, next year, more admits that meet the criteria of the pilot can receive the intervention, growing the impact to a broader number of students. Alternatively, if the pilot was not effective, a new programming initiative can be tested the following cycle. Or something in between. Did a specific population in your pilot respond positively to the intervention? Then you can expand on the nuances you discovered in the pilot. At least staff know more than they did before it was tried. And if we know more each year, then we can serve our students better every year.

That said, establishing clear objectives and defined goals before starting the programming is important. Do you want to increase yield? Or reduce attrition? Or increase GPA? Or increase the knowledge of students? By how much?

How will you measure if the program was successful? These are critical benchmarks to understand as new programming is piloted and then used more broadly at your institution.

Conclusion

The THRIVE Programming strategy enables you to proactively identify and support prospective students through personalized interventions. By assessing Predictive Models and tailoring resources accordingly, you can significantly improve yield rates and student outcomes. This targeted approach not only maximizes the effectiveness of recruitment efforts but also fosters a culture of care and belonging. As a result, students are more likely to succeed and remain engaged, ultimately enriching the academic community and enhancing institutional success.

CHAPTER 20: ENROLLMENTOR - FUTURE DIRECTIONS AND INNOVATIONS

The landscape of CRM technology and data analytics is not only changing quickly, the actual rate of evolution is speeding up. These advancements are both exciting and overwhelming. Especially as the pressure to innovate and improve builds up behind the glacial pace that higher education tends to change.

Change

The important thing to remember is that the changes and improvements you want to make don't have to be perfect this cycle. Every step, pilot, and improvement you make can have a positive and iterative impact on student and institutional success. And you will continue to build momentum, confidence, and experience in these projects, allowing you to continue to move faster.

Sometimes you will move in the wrong direction. Or maybe

sidewise. Or even vaguely meander in a forward-like manner. If the best baseball players in the world strike out 7 out of 10 times at bat, you can give yourself some grace and patience.

Machine Learning

I don't think any conversation about the future can be had without the flashing lights of AI drawing attention. The Predictive Modeling used in this book is relatively manually done. While Slate does automate the model internally, machine learning methods can create powerful models that traditional statistical methods might not be as effective in predicting in comparison.

The prescriptive element of this book remains an extremely impactful tool which is lost in some ML methods. But as ML gets faster, easier, and cheaper, being able to implement several Models can have a profound impact on how institutions operate and support student success.

Generative Ai:

Generative AI like ChatGPT will continue to reshape every aspect of higher education, especially in Admissions. Chatbots, Assistants, and Agents will continue to do the heavy lifting in student interactions - whether that's providing information, guidance, recommendations, support, or even the very act of recruitment.

This will continue to develop into wonderfully curated content that allows for a 1-on-1 pane of glass that allows students to interact with your institution in a way that meets their wants and needs.

Enrollmentor

The role of generative AI will also continue to expand for staff. Whether in understanding information, creating content, or offering recommendations, you're not building a tool. You are spinning up a staff member. A consultant, personal assistant, data scientist, and advisor. You're building an EnrollMentor, providing insight, strategy, and direction at every step of your processes.

I am particularly excited over how AI might augment the strategy and ease of use around Predictive Modeling with recommendations to staff -

- Persona-specific recommendations:
  - Institutional Goal
  - Strategy
  - Action
  - Outcome
  - VPs by default get high-level, short strategy recommendations. Keeps them informed and armed with talking points to Senior Leadership
    - *"To adjust the student body to meet geographic diversity, meet NTR, and improve retention: Increase name buys in Northern California with moderate financial need and high interest in academics. Will increase retention by 1-2%, increase revenue: Year 1 - 47K, Year 2 - 58K... and decrease Admit Rate by 3-5% by Year 3."*
  - Director gets step-by-step effects with % and contingencies
    - *"To meet geographic goals:*
      - *12% more Northern California*
        - *15% College Board*
        - *6% Encoura*
    - *To meet Net Tuition Revenue*
      - *7% decrease of high expected aid*
      - *18% increase in moderate expected aid*
      - *5% increase in low expected aid*

- *Increase retention*
  - *26% increase in Geomarket, neighborhoods, and schools correlated with high interested in academics"*

○ Technical implementers get detailed reports, hyperlinks for their actions, and refreshers/ instruction

- *"Go to collegeboard.com/search*
- *Make these 17 separate search purchases*
  - *Section 1: GPA: A-B+, SAT 1250-1375*
  - *2: Geomarkets: CA 23, Zip Codes: 92408, 92373*
  - *3: etc.*

Data Systems

Institutions will continue generating mountains of data, especially across systems as more of the student's journey is either virtual or at the very least tracked digitally. This can even come in the form of novel types of data to higher education. Eye tracking in portals, engagement cues during tours, etc. These kinds of things feel invasive now, but the last several decades has seen an erosion of privacy and sensitivity in favor of improved experience. It will be interesting to see how the data institutions have access to evolves.

As this reality settles in, systems will optimize for the integration, cleaning, and use of it to drive business processes. AI will also continue to service students and staff throughout their entire tech stack. Whether it's integrating and stitching data, analyzing data, and proactively implementing intervention recommendations.

These systems will also continue improving the student and staff experience while removing friction and technical debt. Delivering information and recruitment through multiple channels and models at any time meets the student where they are in your journey, allowing their relationship to grow with the institution.

Some of the application experience will likely improve as things like transcripts, credentials, and competencies move to more decentralized platforms like blockchain wallets that allow institutions to evaluation the student's knowledge, skills, and abilities in a way that can holistically evaluate their ability to be successful and identify any ways the institution can help them THRIVE. More data moving through your funnels allows you to not only see trends but also evaluate the success of your interventions on those personas.

Much of the work we've covered in this book is applicable to the whole student lifecycle. Whether that's an early alert system for current students or engaging alumni and philanthropy. They can also help the institution engage with current staff and faculty to make their experience better and empower them to find success.

Computation Power

As computers become more powerful and autonomous that opens the door for more complex, powerful and frequent operations. Whether that's creating multidimensional Models and Scoring (subscores for engagement types like MarComm, Social, etc.), more frequent updates for both Scoring and Modeling, including more dynamic and powerful Modeling results, it will do these things while being cheaper, faster, and with less human intervention. This includes more generative AI leading conversations, artisanally curated and personalized MarComms, and recruitment, all geared to increase student and institutional success based on the student's factors and data.

The democratization of these improvements will also allow more institutions of varying sizes and resources to use them, whether that's in house/in system or just more affordable 3rd-party vendors.

A current project I'm working on while writing this book is having Slate generate course registration recommendations based on outstanding class requirements for the student that are available in the upcoming semester. Specific courses with a higher likelihood of academic or post-college success for that student receive special call-outs.

This latter part will become exponentially easier once more current student data is tracked passively and with more computational power behind the behavioral Modeling.

This will extend into other Predictive Models beyond the big ones of enrollment, academic achievement, graduation, giving, etc. As we begin focusing on competencies and aligning the student journey with what they deem to be success, models advancing to things like career pathways can begin to develop.

Conclusion

As you navigate the rapidly evolving landscape of Scoring,

Modeling, and creating experiences in higher education, embracing advancements in data, computing, and AI will become increasingly essential. While these technologies may seem overwhelming, incremental improvements can have significant impacts on student and institutional success. By leveraging generative AI and enhanced data systems, you can create personalized experiences and optimize strategies. The future holds immense potential for more sophisticated models that align with student goals, ultimately fostering success throughout the entire educational journey.

CHAPTER 21: THE CURTAIN CALL

Project

Not only will Scoring and Modeling help you be more strategic, the very act of examining your data and mindfully engaging with your students will improve your process. It's the same with Strategic Enrollment Management. Even if you do not develop a formal SEM plan, just going through the steps and processes will move your practices forward. Even learning the tools and techniques associated with Slate will improve other projects.

There are many reasons Engagement Scoring and Predictive

Modeling can have that direct impact on you and your institutional work. Through understanding your students more deeply and how they interact with your institution, you also start understanding what motivates your students and how you can leverage that knowledge in building more meaningful relationships.

As you foster connections with your students and colleagues, you improve institutional and student success. You will begin interacting better, helping students on their college journey in meaningful and mindful ways. Improving the experience for anyone involved on that journey improves with experience for everyone. And as you incorporate technology in an empowering fashion, you can focus on humans doing the human work that multiplies the benefits this work machines are doing.

You will begin understanding how your funnel operates and how to optimize it to meet your goals and priorities efficiently. This piece becomes more and more important as higher education is feeling the squeeze between moving forward and all of the headwinds pushing us back.

Use

As you leverage TARGET and CRAFT your class, the more you use the data and principles, you optimize that process, improving student and institutional success. And I can attest, the number of cycles you even work on Scoring and Modeling will improve your skills and the very tools as well.

Your ability to not only pull interesting and impactful data will improve, but you will continue to move and track more in your system to inform these processes, improving BEACON data mining at every step of the process.

As your institution becomes more familiar with the variables that influence applying and enrolling, it will also become better at when, how, and who those CTAs work best, making NUDGEs more effective.

The same with GPS guidance. As you start understanding what interactions work best with your different types of students, you not only have the Scores and Models to guide you but a better understanding of the dynamic your counselors and resources have in the relationship. This becomes even more important as you interact with students around those moments that matter like applying after attending an event, stopping engagement after an aid award, and other pivotal intersections.

Probably one of the largest pivots with the longest turning radius is SCOUT recruitment and THRIVE programming. Higher education rarely gets credit as being a nimble industry. And so much money, time, and effort goes into the initiatives around recruitment and programming. But little by little, as you show the impact and ROI of the success (and failures), you can start steering your institution in the best way forward.

Growth

Author's Note: This may or may not be what David feels like whenever he records a The 12 Foot View Video. Go watch them on YouTube to find out for yourself.

Technology continues to advance at a blistering pace. But the concepts in this book, and the support technology can give you, your institution, and the students can act as an EnrollMentor. The less you fight it and the more you embrace it, the more impact you can have. Growth can be uncomfortable, but getting caught in the undergrowth can be suffocating.

As higher education changes, the roles, responsibilities, and required knowledge of staff also changes. Institutions have to invest in their staff. That includes investing in their professional development. This could be in the form of conferences, courses, or even additional time to experiment and learn. Even if an institution implements new technology or adopts new practices, if staff are not able to direct and strategize those processes or at the very least keep up and optimize, then the institution will still fall behind.

I've always valued and prioritized innovation and creativity, and it's been one of my most powerful tools in and out of higher education. These two traits will continue to play pivotal roles as higher education changes and meets students not only where they are, but also where they have to go.

The other lens I've looked through for the projects in this book is being student-centered. Some of the impacts I've painted towards institutional success, but every step of this must be centered around the student, especially what success is in their mind. The student won't be moved because your view of student success is a high GPA and 4 or maybe 6-year graduation. You need to understand who the student is, what motivates them, and what they want from college and life. What is success to them? It's not operationalized in their mind to go to a school with a 90% retention rate.

Epilogue

I've enjoyed writing this book. And I'm sure in even a year, I will have so many updates and revisions that I will need to make to it. And while I do have a couple more books I'd like to write in this series, I'm not sure what cards the future has for me. I did end up getting that job from the TARGET chapter. And while my family isn't growing, I am aware that these are years that a father does not get back. Writing a book is a long time commitment, so if this is my last book, even for now, I'd like to thank you from the bottom of my heart for joining me for it.

There are so many ways institutions are building and using Scores and Models. I am fascinated to continue to learn what's possible and what will be possible. If you'd like to connect, please reach out. Whether you're interested in learning more, taking the next step, or just want to chat about what you're doing. Even if it isn't Scoring or Modeling related. There are many communities this book might touch, and I am interested in the broader work of them all.

I love growing and learning new things. It's one of the reasons I find myself returning to higher education every time. I learned while writing this book. I learned to write this book. And I hope this book has also helped you learn and been a valuable step in your journey.

As the lights dim on our time together, I wish you the best of luck implementing and using Engagement Scores and Predictive Modeling.

ABOUT THE AUTHOR

David Dysart

David's experience includes, IR, Admission, Enrollment Management, and Consulting while at large public, liberal arts, and private research universities, as well as a firm. He is happy to have refound his home in higher ed and especially happy to be here with you today.

LinkedIn: https://www.linkedin.com/in/daviddysart/

YouTube -
Engagement Scoring and Predictive Modeling: https://tinyurl.com/AdmissionWorkshops

The 12-Foot View: https://tinyurl.com/The12FootView

Email: DysArtisanalInnovations@gmail.com

www.ingramcontent.com/pod-product-compliance
Lightning Source LLC
LaVergne TN
LVHW051732050326
832903LV00023B/892